Meetings,
Meetings and
MORE Meetings

Meetings,
Meetings and
MORE Meetings

Getting Things Done
When People Are Involved

SIMON RAMO, Ph.D.

BONUS BOOKS
Los Angeles, California

The illustrations in this book were created by Tim Heidrich from
rough sketches by the author.

09   08   07   06   05   5   4   3   2   1

Ramo, Simon.
   Meetings, meetings and more meetings : getting things done
when people are involved /. by Simon Ramo.
       p. cm.
   ISBN 1-56625-256-3
   1. Business meetings. I. Title.
   HF5734.5.R36   2004
   658.4'56—dc22
                                              2005011367

Bonus Books
1223 Wilshire Blvd. #597
Santa Monica, CA 90403

Printed in the United States of America

To Virginia,
most beautiful of Meeting-Goer-Toers.

Contents

Meetings, Meetings, and More Meetings

After a day of going to one meeting after another, some stressful, some boring, some both, I found myself at a dinner sitting next to a lady I had not previously met. Right away she asked me what I did; without thinking I told her, "I go to meetings."

"I beg your pardon," she responded. "You do what?"

"I go to meetings. I'm a professional meeting-goer-toer."

"That's a profession?" she asked.

"Oh, yes" I answered quickly. "It takes skill and experience. I have both. I'm an expert at meeting-going-toing," I went on, realizing that my frivolous remarks tossed off as a thoughtless reaction to an annoying question had some sense to them and that I might have stumbled on to something.

"I have written the definitive textbook on the Principles of Meeting-Going-Toing," I mischievously added, surprising myself by relaxing and beginning to enjoy the conversation.

That claim I made was not truthful then, but it is now. This is that text.

After acquiring an education, getting a job and settling into it, huge chunks of our working life are spent arranging, preparing for, going to, chairing, participating in, avoiding, canceling, rescheduling, and sometimes dozing through *Meetings*. Of course, many hours a day are also devoted to phone conversations, faxes, e-mails, memos, conference calls, and surfing the web. But when you are running any kind of organization, a meeting is the principal vehicle by which the attendees create plans, reach decisions, formulate directives, and perform critical communicating.

The nation's productivity cannot be optimized if graduates in business administration, law, economics, engineering, education, political science, and the rest leave academics and go to work ignorant of the one skill that they will be required to utilize the most. Yet no university lists in its course catalogue "Introduction to Meeting-Going-Toing" or "Meetings 101—Theory and Practice." Some would argue that this shortcoming proves that lack of practical realism and pioneering zeal characterizes the leaders of higher education; I think the real answer may be that there is no available textbook—hence I decided to produce one.

A Primer At Last

I would be exaggerating if I said that this book presents meeting-going-toing as an intellectual discipline—it would be more accurately described as the textbook for a hypothetical college course. This course would prepare students for what will be a significant portion of their life's employment, meetings. I would be surprised however, if even with this text now in print, such a course is ever offered (the potential teachers of it may be too busy attending meetings). In any case, I hope that people who have had to become regular meeting attendees will find this book of interest; surely some professional meeting-goer-toers must sense they are missing a definitive statement of what constitutes their profession. I hope this book will provide for them a theoretical foundation, a finishing touch, to perfect their real-life-developed expertise in meeting-going-toing.

Marvelous accomplishments, we know, can result when unusual individuals work alone. Mozart harmonizing, Einstein conceiving, Picasso visualizing, Heifetz perfecting, Edison lighting, and Shakespeare playing—many examples come to mind. But even these geniuses had to meet with others—peers, backers, implementers, critics, sympathizers, communicators, and agents—or their creations would not have received their deserved attention. Of course, not everyone is a creative genius, and most people are busy with less inspiring tasks handed down by their supervisors. Those toiling alone are often engaged in assembling material to be used in meetings, and most lone contributors provide a supportive function for those who run things. It is the latter, it appears, who are unable to perform their roles without frequent face-to-face interaction with others.

Even in the cave-dwelling period of mankind a dictatorial tribal chieftain could not manage everything going on without conferring with others. Take Uggar[1] for example. Did he simply issue orders, which the tribe then obediently followed? No, Uggar actually called several powwows a day to announce his directives and see they were being obeyed. He typically quizzed the invitees to obtain working knowledge (as to what was accomplished on the hunt he ordered, for instance, or for news about nearby unfriendly tribes). Those were the earliest known examples of meetings.

Why So Many Meetings

Still, why are so many meetings held these days? Every would-be success story needs time to ponder privately and peacefully; how can the doers of the world tolerate a corporate structure that leaves them so few hours to themselves? Modern technology allows "virtual" meetings, which would seem to have all the benefits and few of the drawbacks of a physical meeting. If you do have an actual meeting then the modern technological aids available to you should increase the volume, speed, and breadth of acquiring, refining, storing, and disseminating information. With more processed

---

[1] I have invented Uggar. All other individuals cited in this book are based on actual people I have observed whose names I have altered for the usual reasons and whose true characteristics I have sometimes combined with the patterns of others to create fictitious individuals helpful in making points.

data readily provided to more people, more of them are enabled to act effectively, so meetings should be better run, cover more pertinent territory, and reach more useful conclusions earlier. Shouldn't the full application of these modern info systems diminish the volume of needed meetings?

Not really. It turns out that with more recipients of more information, more questions, opinions, and ideas are generated. So more meetings have to take place to work out the differences. Moreover, the speed-up offered by the new information systems causes new difficulties because the personnel involved have to endeavor to stay apace. Added meetings must be scheduled to enable following up on the accelerated info flow.

Many years ago I was on the board of a large hospital that had to fire Adams, a top executive. When Adams had first come on staff he had looked sensational because he was such an expert in computer systems. In those days all the information to run the hospital—patients' medical records, scheduling, payrolls, billing, ordering, and inventory flow—were in separate filing systems, none readily accessed. Adams changed that so everyone could get any data anywhere in the whole hospital at any of the numerous personal computers he installed. Adams was so proud of this he did not notice that many of the staff were accessing, and becoming involved in, topics well beyond their competence and responsibility. As the hospital staff started to get bogged down in Adams' ever increasing data flow he failed to see that productivity was going down. He remained unaware of the fact that meetings were proliferating all over the hospital in an attempt to coordinate the increased participation of more people in more functions.

In order for workers to get things done a reasonably harmonious ensemble of duties is needed. No substitute for person-to-person meetings has been invented because conference calls, faxed pie charts, and e-mails don't disclose facial expressions and body language. They don't show the reaction of one person to what another has said; whether that reaction is positive: nods, winks, and smiles of acceptance, or negative: the frowns, grimaces, head wagging, bristling and the throwing up of hands in disgust. Humans have an overpowering desire to know what others are thinking. Meetings are demanded by the genes of Homo Sapiens because it is

Common Phrases of Meeting-Going-Toers

"I guess you know why I called you all together"

"I suppose you're wondering why I called you all together"

"Let's try to put a meeting together"

"Why can't we meet later?"

"Why can't we meet earlier?"

"Why can't we meet here?"

"Why don't we take that up at the meeting?"

"Here's what we'll do at the meeting"

"I'll explain it at the meeting"

"Sorry—I have to hang up—I'm late for a meeting"

"I've already got a meeting that morning"

"Everything has to be ready in time for the meeting"

"The meeting won't decide anything"

"The meeting should never have been held"

"You mean you didn't go to the meeting?"

"This can't be our last meeting"

"I doubt I'll be invited to the next meeting"

"Why wasn't I included in the meeting?"

"Who said a meeting was necessary?"

"If I were you I would set up a meeting"

"If I were you I wouldn't go to the meeting"

"If I were you I would cancel the meeting"

"Why do we need another meeting?"

"So when's our next meeting?"

only when we meet that we can receive a full range of signals from each other.

Take Mrs. Hill, who chaired a monthly meeting I used to attend. Her eyeball movements and the rise and fall of her eyelids and eyebrows told me much more than even her lengthiest response to a comment of mine. Our species have powers of intuition and mind reading. Mrs. Hill at least, surely possessed those gifts. As others presented data and opinions or ideas, I had only to watch Mrs. Hill's face—as we all did—to know which she believed, doubted, or thought ridiculous. Mrs. Hill was very influential on the issues about which we met and it was extremely valuable in a meeting to learn quickly what Mrs. Hill was thinking.

There is much more to human communication than words and numbers. People want to see directly whether others are confident, or doubtful, worried, tired, angry, disgusted, tense, disappointed, surprised, happy, sad, determined, alert, or about to doze off. In any kind of interaction with others we need all senses to be operating in full gear in order to be confident we are communicating.

Putting Heads Together

"Two heads are better than one" is a familiar saying; but it isn't true if the two disagree on everything and hate rather than respect each other. The two heads are even more ineffectual when they are incompatible *and* share responsibilities. A more accurate saying may be that multiple heads are only better than one if they have been properly teamed. A deeply ingrained pessimist may present a severe problem to a highly optimistic partner, and vice versa. But, if the two are assigned to assist a wise, experienced head who has decision authority, then the three could constitute a very successful task force. The "boss" will possess a wide coverage of alternatives to consider when both positive and negative potentials surface, this making for far sounder decisions than one mind alone could achieve.

A highly successful meeting assembled to discuss a complex problem or opportunity is a "meeting of minds." If the issues the meeting is dealing with are multidimensional, then the inclusion of many specialist attendees will be mandatory. But the meeting participants will also have to include those whose skills and experiences are of an integrating nature. Such "systems" thinkers will relate the efforts of the detailed specialists to the overall result being sought. The separate contributions then will be synthesized into a compatible whole that attains the meeting's objectives.

Many meetings are called to generate ideas and a well thought out mix of participants is essential. Practical people who know how to get things done must be present, but these types are rarely creative as well. If they have little imagination and are not innovative, their brains must be coupled with those spewing original thoughts. These originators, in turn, may lack the ability to assess what will and won't work in practice. Combining varied brain power is the answer.

When ingenious minds are in each other's presence each of them rises to a higher level of ingenuity. One innovator may have only the beginning of an approach to a problem, but another, hearing that beginning, is inspired to come up with another essential piece. This idea augmentation process is evident in a wide range of meetings: engineers seeking a way of satisfying a design requirement, professional wits plotting a comedy program, lawyers and accountants seeking how to minimize taxes. Conceivers are moved to top other originators interacting with them. Putting heads together is a short way of describing what successful meetings really do.

Pressure for Meetings

Meetings are generally called because numerous circumstances produce pressure for calling them. For example, the increasing ease of international travel and trends towards globalization have combined to make it attractive and possible for corporate activities to cover larger geographical areas. At the same time, the ways of the world are becoming more complex by the day. Managers now have to consider the rules, traditions and cultures of multiple nations. Executives all over the world feel an increasing need for person-to-person contact and can meet within hours after deciding to do so. The conferring that managers need in order to perform well reflects these changes. More things to consider mean more meetings to consider them and, naturally, more meetings to prepare for the considering of them.

The more widespread and multifaceted an activity becomes, the harder it is to tie all the separate pieces together. Hence management failures are more probable, unless person-to-person meetings are well planned and numerous. Interestingly, opportunities to be creative in management methods also grow. The technology not only makes it possible to run things better, but more information moving to innovative individuals excites them to do more innovating. But most meeting-goer-toers are likely to become so swamped as they attend to the myriad of interactions that they can easily miss the spotting of opportunities. So meetings have to be set up particularly to increase creativity.

Another stimulator of meetings in our age is the phenomenon of increasing specialization. The more complex a situation the greater is the need for specialized experts to deal with its many facets and the greater the tendency for the required expertise to keep breaking into ever more levels of yet more detailed specialization. The wider the resulting spectrum of specialists, the narrower and ever deeper becomes each added specialty. Then it becomes even more important to meet and relate the increased range of specialization one to another and ensure a cohesive whole.

Unnecessary Meetings

We have all attended meetings that were either redundant or unnecessary; generally the pointlessness of such a meeting is realized only after it has been called and held.[2] A needless meeting may get set up because the Chair or someone else influential enough to schedule the meeting simply makes a mistake. Hawkins, who chaired the board of a charity on which I served, erred often. He had the bad habit of calling "special" meetings in addition to the

---

[2] We shall only mention, but not elaborate on, annual tax-deductible expense-covered "meetings" called by business executives, physicians, bankers, tax lawyers, etc. to places like Hawaii, Hong Kong, Bermuda, or Venice, Italy. Cleveland is never chosen.

regularly scheduled ones. Hawkins sincerely believed that every problem he noticed needed immediate attention, but when everyone gathered to solve it, the group would realize it would be best to hand it to a specialist in that field. Or else the topic of the meeting belonged on the agenda of some other committee whose meeting was already scheduled. This over-calling of meetings was due to a lack of adequate knowledge by Hawkins as to what was going on. Sometimes the special meeting he called would have made sense had it been scheduled for later, following a study not yet completed. Another habit of Hawkins was to continue to call meetings for a particular project—one that once needed talent and time intensive meetings—long after the necessity of calling them had ended.

I came to hope for Hawkins' early retirement. When he showed no sign of accommodating me I resigned from that board.

Another reason for excessive meetings are individuals who "collect" them. Professor Landers is typical of this class of meeting-goer-toer. He never heard of a meeting he didn't want to attend. The more meetings Landers is invited to, the happier he is. If he hears about a meeting to which he was not invited, he wonders why and feels hurt. He schemes daily to be asked to participate and, inevitably, he does everything he can to cause new meetings to be called, needed or not. Landers cultivates and joins with others like himself. Together they elevate the promotion of meetings to a reason for living.

Unnecessary Committees

Still another reason for unnecessary meetings is the number of unnecessary committees. If a problem, opportunity, threat, or need arises, the tradition in America is to appoint a committee to investigate and recommend a solution. That committee then has to meet, and when it meets it usually leads to additional committees being formed and meetings being called to ponder issues that will have arisen in that first meeting.

Political organizations are forever creating "advisory councils" to raise electioneering funds which in turn call scores of unnecessary meetings. Usually the organizers seek to interest you by claiming a desperate need for your advice. They feed your ego by asking you to attend a "high-level" meeting where only you and others like you have been invited. These lucky invitees are all very prominent folks, they would have you believe, all experts, and of high character and motivation; all judged by the inviters to be able to write a generous check for political support. Raising money for election campaigns is essential to keep government machinery operating, so these meetings are necessary. But the fact that the true criterion for invitations is hidden (even if everyone knows why they are attending) shows that the process needs improvement and a more effective substitute for these political meetings is needed. But don't bet that this will happen.

Universities set up lots of advisory committees. The Music School, Medical School, Engineering School, and the rest each create such a group. It is called a "Board of Counselors" or some other impressive name. Rarely do these boards provide useful advice and the advice usually is not even sought. The members are appointed not because they might render valuable counseling but rather because they are thought capable of financial aid to the University. Thus the Medical School's advisory board's agenda always includes presentations by the School's leading researchers to show what remarkable new cures their research might generate if only it were adequately funded—which it never is. The meeting makes clear that the only acceptable course of action is for the board members to contribute money.

Some committees are eminently sensible. Their recommendations contribute to effective progress. But happy results will occur only if additional meetings are scheduled to explore how to act on those recommendations. The planned actions will then need to be coordinated and judged in further meetings.

Reports Lead to Meetings

Studies and reports are a permanent part of American corporate life. The greater the number of printed reports issued, the greater the likelihood that those who receive the reports will feel the need for holding meetings about them. This will sometimes happen for reports no one has had the time or interest to scan. A report may not be read but can nevertheless give rise to a "should have read it" syndrome. The best example that I have ever observed of devoted meeting-goer-toers with this affliction was Dickerson. My coworkers and I quickly gathered that Dickerson never actually read a report. I don't know exactly why that happened, because Dickerson constantly pressed his associates for comments about individual reports that crossed his desk. "Have you read it?" he would inquire of everyone. He always opined that the report he was asking about sounded very interesting and that he would read it as soon as he got back to his office. If someone, most often in response to his avid questioning, mentioned some report he had not seen, he would send for a copy.

Why did we suspect Dickerson never read reports? Because in every meeting he arranged to discuss a report, Dickerson's questions would indicate total unfamiliarity with the report's key issues. My theory was that it was on his conscience that he had not done his homework; he had not done right by the report. So he would decide to make it up to the report writer and announce that the report merited a meeting.

Of course, some circulated reports actually are useful and get studied by the right people. This almost always leads to meetings specifically to discuss doing something about the important things those reports have uncovered. Reports usually make a case for further study, the resulting meetings confirm this need, and in turn, that becomes a reason for demanding forthcoming report extensions. If reports beget meetings, meetings more or less equally give birth to reports. The meeting in other words, leads to offspring meetings that produce more meetings themselves. The result is an explosion in meetings. Information technology magnifies the process because it causes more people to receive copies of more reports. Some of that enlarged group then actually read the reports, causing them to see reasons for new meetings to consider what should be done in view of the reported situations.

Abolishing the Unnecessary

How can you help abolish unnecessary meetings? One way is not to go to them. You can't pull that off every time, of course, because you may get fired, as happened to my friend Eaton. Eaton decided to skip meetings called by his boss whenever he believed them to be unnecessary. Finally he did exactly that for a meeting the boss had called with Eaton alone.

When you are invited to a meeting you are certain will accomplish nothing, ask yourself whether you have choices. You might phone the Chair or someone that is influential in regards to that meeting and explain why you believe it should be cancelled. In the ensuing discussion you may discover, of course, that you were way off in your assessment. On the other hand you might be successful in canceling the meeting if he or she agrees with you; this may even work with bosses. You might get credit with them for having the guts to say why the meetings they are calling are better cancelled. However, be ready to resign if you aren't able to suggest a better way to resolve the problem the boss called that meeting to deal with. Maybe you can argue convincingly that the issue should simply be assigned to a certain person to handle alone, or that it should be added to the agenda of an already established meeting. Perhaps you have additional information that suggests the problem should be ignored because it will go away of it's own accord.

Suppose everyone in an operating entity of substantial size believes that too many meetings are being held. Someone is then sure to suggest that a meeting be called for the purpose of discussing ways to cut down on the number of meetings. This new meeting will hopefully identify meetings that can be cancelled or consolidated. Lawrence, one of the few meeting-goer-toers I knew well who was vocal about there being too many meetings, tried this. Alas, Lawrence's efforts caused an increase in the number of meetings. You see, his very first meeting, which he chaired and I attended, listed some existing regular meetings as candidates for abolishment. Within minutes we got into controversies about whether this or that particular meeting was truly essential or should be eliminated. The only way to settle these differences seemed to be to hold added meetings.

Success in a meeting reduction effort has to end with more meetings being cancelled than are spawned by the reduction effort.

The Meeting Imperative

Resisting attempts to decrease the number of meetings is part of the culture of meeting-goer-toers. They become accustomed to lives dominated by meetings. Going to meetings every day and knowing that a full schedule of meetings stretches out into the future lends security, purpose, and continuity to their beings. Arriving at the office in the morning only to discover there is no scheduled meeting for that day leaves them lost and confused.

This condition once lasted a week for meeting-goer-toer Rucker. On a Monday Rucker discovered no meeting was on his calendar for that day, or for Tuesday or Wednesday. By Friday panic set in. Months passed before Rucker fully recovered his confidence. When his mental health returned Rucker was determined to arrange enough future meetings to guarantee no hiatus would ever again occur. Rucker at first assumed he had only to employ a simple equation: For every meeting he attended, one future meeting needed scheduling. This was easy because a meeting typically produces adequate evidence that a future meeting is necessary. Usually that next meeting is set before the current meeting adjourns. Should this not happen, Rucker figured he simply had to take the initiative after every meeting to engineer a new meeting on some topic or other.

But these steps proved inadequate because of the associated phenomena of meeting cancellations. To compensate for the inevitable cancellations, Rucker discovered that the number of his planned future meetings must exceed substantially the number of meetings that actually take place. In order to ensure that every day had a meeting, Rucker's Rule eventually became that for every meeting attended a meeting-goer-toer should set up a *minimum* of two future meetings.

You don't have to be Einstein to figure out why so many scheduled meetings are cancelled. Date conflicts can often be resolved if a meeting involves only a small group of attendees. But as the number of attendees and the number of meetings they each attend are increased, they usually will have made previous commitments on the possible dates for the proposed meeting. The negotiation effort required increases exponentially making the scheduling process for a new meeting more and more difficult. Each potential member becomes available to attend the proposed new meeting only if some other meeting already posted for that date can be rescheduled; one meeting date negotiation can give rise to numerous rescheduling of numerous other meetings. So a chain of rescheduling is born and it acquires added links in a hurry. Out-and-out cancellations will then result because of inability to find dates that will work for enough of the required attendees.

Study of Meeting-Going-Toing

With so much meeting-going-toing going on, and the likelihood of more to come, one hardly needs an excuse to justify studying the process with a view to improving it. In my own long career I estimate I have attended over forty thousand meetings. (That's only an average of two or three meetings a day for seventy years—I'm now in my nineties.) Those meetings I've attended have involved many diverse activities: business management, scientific research, higher education, government advisories, charitable foundations, Little League, symphony and opera boards, weapons systems projects, etc. That is a lot of meetings with a lot of different people, yet I recall that only a few meeting-going-toers ever took serious action to improve meetings, such as shortening overly lengthy meetings or cutting down on unnecessary scheduling. Regrettably, I don't remember a single attendee ever questioning the entire process of meeting-going-toing, even though such an effort might have led to the reduction of the bad and enhancement of the good elements of meetings.

In the chapters to follow we shall continue the pondering of meeting-going-toing this chapter has begun. As each chapter probes more meeting characteristics, it is hoped the reader will become convinced—as is the author—that the structure or meetings can be enhanced. Unnecessary meetings can be minimized and the goings on when conferring takes place can be made more beneficial. Of course, the reader may not agree. So with the goal of making the next edition of this text more convincing, I would hope to gather readers' opinions after they have finished reading it. To accomplish that I may need to call a meeting.

Agendas: Yours and Everyone Else's

Every meeting has an agenda, and the topics covered in a meeting may hinge on the pushiness of the attendees in working out that agenda. The agenda is not merely the typed program sheet showing the planned timing and order of topics to be taken up in the meeting. That agenda usually sits conspicuously in front of the Chair with copies before the rest of the attendees. It may have been distributed ahead of time to increase the likelihood that the participants will prepare properly for the meeting. Such an agenda is overt—it is intended to be known by all—and that is all we need say about it. We shall concentrate instead on the other agendas, the covert ones; those most folks would call the "hidden agendas." There is guaranteed to be more on the minds of the meeting-goers than is disclosed by a list of meeting topics. All serious meeting-going-toers will arrive at the meeting with secret strategies they will have devised in an attempt to achieve certain aims from the meeting. If you as an attendee are going to indulge in such strategy creation, and you definitely should, then you ought to do it right. That's what this chapter will be about.

The Covert Agenda

Let's begin with an example. Mary, an outstanding meeting-going-toing veteran, is mulling over a coming meeting of the board of trustees of her state's college system. Several colleges make up the system, each headed by a president who reports to the chancellor who is the chief executive over the whole. Hamilton, the board chairman, has called a meeting to choose a new chancellor, the present one retiring soon.

As an accomplished pro, Mary starts her preparation for the meeting by identifying some questions. Who will attend the meeting? What will be the various attendees' objectives? What are their degrees of expertise and biases in regards to the meeting's purpose? Who likely will make presentations seeking what effects? Is the get-together, as she hopes, likely to focus on studying the candidates and settling on one? Or will the other participants, all following their own agendas, cause the meeting to adjourn without reaching a decision? Will they agree on what to do next?

Most importantly, what is Mary's own agenda? What specific meeting conclusions does she favor? How can she bring about the result she wants? To answer these questions she may have to do some research before the meeting. She might call a few small meetings herself to gather necessary information. She is an expert at all this, however, very quick at asking herself the right questions and at researching, pondering, and formulating plans.

Mary decides right away that Wrigley, who presently heads the largest college in the state's system, will be a problem. She is sure he would love to become chancellor. But he did not make the trustees' list, or the faculty's list, or the roster of candidates recommended by the outside search firm the board hired. (Had he been so named he naturally would not have been invited to this meeting.) He was ruled out because at sixty he is ten years older than the ideal age of fifty already set.

In contrast, another president, Fletcher, is a finalist on everyone's list. Now forty-eight, he has been regularly rated superb in every way: academic stature, managerial competence, personality, leadership qualities, and political savvy. Wrigley clearly is extremely jealous of Fletcher. Mary knows Wrigley will try to plant doubts about Fletcher with the trustees. He will press for the appointment of the weakest possible chancellor, someone he might hope to bully and control. Wrigley also will hope no strong candidate will accept if asked and the trustees will come to him after all, despite his age.

The trustees are all political appointees of the governor of the State. With her as the lone exception, she knows they understand little of the problems of running colleges. They take pride in being trustees, honorariums bestowed on them by governors in return for their having been generous donors to those governors' political campaigns. They will not try to anticipate, as she does, what other attendees might be thinking and saying during the meeting's discussions. Thus, ill-prepared, they will not deliver their own thoughts well or counter effectively recommendations they might not like when presented by others.

The chairman, Hamilton, she knows, has serious ambitions to run for governor himself when the present governor finishes his term. Hamilton will greatly prefer a chancellor with political skill whom he can use as a valuable aid when he seeks that office. Trustee Kimball will also be a special case deserving her attention. He is the biggest landowner in his part of the state and thus one of its most powerful figures. He wants an additional state college to be created in the center of his vast holdings, something that would greatly increase his lands' value. Other trustees may ask for serious consideration of individuals they will already have pushed onto the early candidate lists—associates and others suggested by sources having axes to grind. Mary knows she will need to be alert to challenge such names quickly if they are introduced.

Who will be the most credible trustee in pressing for the right candidate to be chosen? She will be, she concludes. She is now the longest serving trustee, the only trustee with a Ph.D. degree, and the only one who has been a professor at a major university. She knows why she was appointed to the board despite having no political connections; her first book, one in a hugely successful series of biographies of the nation's first ladies, was *Bess, Mamie, and Pat;* it sold over a million copies and was uniformly praised by critics. This was followed by the definitive book on Eleanor Roosevelt that was an even bigger seller and caused Mary to become a well known public figure. The governor who appointed Mary realized it was time to add a trustee who was highly knowledgeable in higher education. He further realized that Mary could be used to make public statements lauding the college system's performance and explaining its needs and that, as a sort of celebrity, her remarks would interest the media and the public. Indeed, since her appointment she has substantially improved the system's funding.

Mary decides Fletcher should be the next chancellor. Conceivably some other candidate she doesn't know at all might be superior. But she decides that is unlikely, and to pick an unknown is an unnecessary risk. In the meeting she will make herself the chief proponent for Fletcher's selection.

How should Mary persuade chairman Hamilton to support her proposal? She decides to make a little speech early in the meeting about Fletcher's having excellent political skills and argue that he can be counted on to lobby the legislature successfully for support for the college system. She knows that Hamilton will now join her in recommending Fletcher because, as she speaks, Hamilton will inevitably come up with the idea of exploiting Fletcher's political savvy to aid his campaign for governor.

How will she sell Kimball on Fletcher? By promising him her backing for his desired new college if he will support her nomination of Fletcher.

Mary is ready now to go to the meeting. She has decided what result she wants. She knows what her role will be. She has her agenda.

Is Mary's way of preparing for a meeting a good model for meeting-goer-toers? For some, yes. Of course, not all people have Mary's self-confidence (bordering on conceit, a common characteristic of influential meeting participants). Nor can everyone possess her knowledge of the players and her wisdom about the meeting's purpose. All in all, however, the way Mary went about the matter of inventing her secret strategy for the meeting sets a good example.

The New Attendees

The heart and details of one's hidden agenda depend, of course, on one's relation to the meeting's subjects, to the other attendees, and to the meeting's Chair. Suppose you are a young person attending your first meeting; is it a good rule for neophyte meeting attendees to avoid overly aggressive participation? If you are a new member should you speak only when called on by the Chair or some highly respected member? No. Even if doing so was a good idea, following this rule is often easier said than done. Your presence may have been requested in order to offset the unwanted dullness expected of the meeting. Maybe you are thought to be capable of offering new, bold, uninhibited ideas to add zip to the discussion and prevent emphasis on trite, out-of-date approaches. By being hesitant and shy you might disappoint.

I had a set of experiences early in my career that illustrates this well. My first real job after completing my university education was in research and development (R&D) at General Electric. I arrived there in 1936, the seventh year of The Great Depression. By that time many companies across the country had folded. GE, the largest electrical company in the world, was surviving but by that time the executives chosen to set company policy were not of the imaginative, risk-taking kind. The precarious economics situation of that period naturally caused cautious leadership to be put in command.

As will soon become evident I was the youngest and most immature of the scientists and engineers that comprised GE's R&D team at that time, especially when it came to matters such as industry management, corporate finance, the national economy, and the principles of meeting-going-toing. At lunch each day the staff's informal cafeteria discussions centered on the company's R&D budgets and its goals for creating new high technology products. We argued about company policies or lack of them to encourage science and technology advances. Almost immediately I developed the reputation of being unhesitantly outspoken. I felt strongly that GE's policy of very careful—I thought stingy—allocation of resources was holding back the pace of R&D.

I argued GE would lose its world leadership in the electrical field if it did not go after all the potential developments of the new and evolving sciences. I knew nothing at that time about GE's cash flow, its available assets, its debt to equity ratio, its profit and loss figures, or its balance sheet. It never occurred to me that I was an ignoramus about such issues. But older staff members who were not getting the support they wanted for their R&D efforts were developing the habit of dropping in on me in my lab. They apparently needed someone, even if young, who would readily commiserate sympathetically with them.

One day the oldest researcher in the laboratories visited me. He told me everyone enjoyed my readily offered criticism of company policies but that I needed to be more careful and should quiet down. When he left I was convinced I should follow his advice to the letter. I really did not know much about anything beyond some aspects of science and technology. How could I not have realized that? I must have appeared to be presumptuous, an ignorant upstart who should not be speaking out on matters of general management, especially in so difficult a business period. My adviser was a kind, gentle old man, distinguished in his field. He didn't actually say that I didn't know what I was talking about and should shut up. But I got the message. I resolved to change my role in lunchtime conversations.

The next meeting I attended was called by the head of the laboratory, and not surprisingly I conducted myself carefully and was very subdued, and acted accordingly to the fatherly advice I had recently received. I had assumed it would be a big meeting of the entire R&D staff because otherwise I, a junior, would not have been on the head's list. In any event, I did not ask myself why I was invited and I never thought to prepare myself for the meeting. I simply showed up.

I was amazed to find that the meeting was small. As I looked around I saw that the other attendees were senior people and I was the only young researcher present. Thank Heavens, I said to myself, that I had had the good fortune to be counseled only a week earlier about my too openly critical nature. I could have sounded off at this meeting and been seen as a sassy, immature fool! I might even have been fired!

It turned out that the meeting was about planning the R&D program. The big boss started the discussion with two things: the total money available for R&D in the period ahead, and a listing of areas of R&D to pursue showing his priorities and proposed allocations of funds. He then sought comments from the group. As soon as I sensed this meeting plan I decided I should say nothing unless clearly called upon. Even then, I planned to agree with the plan and offer no changes and no criticisms. If called upon I would be very brief; I would show maturity and defer to the older and wiser people in the room. I would prove I had the common sense to realize I was too inexperienced to make meaningful comments on the subject of the meeting.

I was not called on and I ended up saying nothing in that conference. I was proud of having become sensible. I had learned how to handle myself in meetings with more experienced people.

But I was wrong. The very next morning I got a call to come to the head's office—and this time the meeting comprised him and me! He said he had made a mistake in bringing me into the meeting the day before without telling me why ahead of time. He should have realized, he said, that I would be hesitant to speak my mind in the presence of so many elders. But, he went on to explain, he had particularly wanted to get some reactions to the plan for the labs from the "younger generation." Lab hiring, he pointed out, had been halted for several years and so there were few of what he called "the next generation." Moreover, he told me he had heard I had voiced interesting comments on occasion that indicated a lack of full admiration for GE's R&D program.

Not only did I feel free to speak up but it was clear that my boss was actually ordering me to respond. I immediately called attention to the way the previous day's meeting had started, namely, with a predetermined figure for the total R&D budget. Where did that number come from I asked? Who decided it? Why did everyone at the meeting accept it as correct and unchangeable? Perhaps the number was too small, I offered carefully.

My naiveté must have amused him because he smiled in response, but we went on to have what was for me a marvelous and fascinating session. My boss not only smiled throughout our talk but engaged me in a vibrant give and take exchanges of ideas and opinions. I learned from that meeting much more than he did. But I think he got what he wanted.

Why You?

What did I learn from this episode? Firstly, I should have asked myself why I was invited to the initial meeting. If I had done so, I might have prepared to play my role. I should also have considered: What is the meeting about? Such questions should be routine for every meeting-goer-toer, because they are essential to the creating of (hidden) agendas. Consider the two or three most probable reasons why you might have been invited, then prepare for each one. During the meeting watch the Chair for clues. Are the Chair or other people looking at you when a particular subject or question comes up? Maybe they invited you to the meeting in order to size you up. Perhaps the Chair, also a high executive in the management hierarchy, wants to see if you have viewpoints worth considering and the ability to express and defend them when others challenge you. It could be you are a prospect for advancement and your performance may determine your next career step.

There are many different types of meetings, and not all require you to devise an agenda. For example, you may be invited to a big meeting where all that is required is to listen to a single presentation. In this situation consider whether there will be a period for questioning the speaker; will you be expected to question or even challenge him? Will you be judged a disappointing dullard if you don't participate or, will you make a fool of yourself or be thought a pushy grandstander if you get into the act? Your chosen hidden agenda may range from one needing virtually no effort ahead of the meeting to one requiring serious, extensive homework for its creation. If you fail to recognize the value of pre-meeting consideration of your secret agenda you will disqualify yourself for the status of a competent professional meeting-goer-toer.

Machiavellian Agendas

MACHIAVELLI HAS HIS OWN AGENDA

Meetings are critical to their participants and the atmosphere within them reflects this; some attendees will feel threatened, and tensions and emotions will run close to the surface. A meeting can make or break careers and the budgets, policies, and plans decided upon can cause job losses for thousands of employees. Hopes and dreams can be born or shattered in meetings and each attendees' performance during the meeting can have serious consequences for him or her.

No wonder then that experienced meeting-goer-toers come to meetings with hidden agendas that they have carefully crafted. It is understood that the participants—all humans with needs, ambitions, and concerns—may use wiles during meetings. Animals may use cunning to protect themselves or get what they want, but our higher species can excel in sophisticated trickery, feints, bluffs, and stealth. Machiavelli showed how to do this in *The Prince*, and most of what he wrote can be useful to someone seeking to have an impact in a meeting today.

It might appear that I am recommending that you need to create a secret agenda and become an expert at gambits and knavery. Not exactly. Machiavelli's treatise tells how to acquire and keep power—but its methods require you to be cunning. Thus if you behave in meetings as Machiavelli recommends you may not be invited to future meetings. Determining what kind of meeting conduct is ethical and what is wrong is not always a simple matter, and there is a bit of Machiavelli in each of us. Right or wrong, when people come together to deal with subjects important to them, they may well act Machiavellian under the strain. It is naïve to assume people will not act this way, or to fail to detect this behavior immediately should it take place during a meeting, or to think Machiavellian conduct never succeeds. To be naïve will put you at a disadvantage. We cite examples.

A gentleman, call him Salisbury, happened to be Chair of the membership committee of a certain exclusive club. As Chair, he had the privilege of setting the dates of committee meetings when the votes were taken on new member candidates. Salisbury was anxious to get his good friend Ryan, an attorney, accepted for membership at a coming meeting, but knew there would be a problem with Davis. Davis was another lawyer and a membership committee member and he hated Ryan. (Ryan had defeated Davis in a recent tough legal battle.) When Ryan's name came up for preliminary consideration at an earlier meeting, Davis had made highly negative comments. One blackball would be sufficient to eliminate Ryan as a potential club member.

Now, Salisbury had originally scheduled the next membership committee meeting for the tenth of the month but then learned that on the twelfth Davis would be out of town for a major performance in a highly publicized court case. So on the ninth Salisbury cancelled the meeting for the tenth and rescheduled it for the twelfth. When Davis returned and learned Ryan was voted in during his absence he was furious, but his anger was futile. Salisbury clearly had been Machiavellian, but in his mind Davis was the real misbehaver because he sought to keep a good new member out for wrong reasons.

Now imagine that an unabashed Machiavelli is attending a conference where a matter important to him will be decided. What would Mr. Machiavelli do to steer the meeting's activity toward his desired outcome?

First, he will attempt to get the right person to be the Chair of the meeting. If the big boss will chair the meeting, and there is no choice as to that, he will concentrate on the other attendees, using the Chair to help him. Machiavelli will seek to do this without the Chair being fully aware of it—something he will hope to be successful at because he will reckon he is smarter than the Chair. Machiavelli is very determined and focused and he is not hesitant about being manipulative. He will use his focused determination and willingness to manipulate to try to remove anyone he suspects will push the wrong way in the meeting from the invitees' list. Machiavelli will accomplish this by confiding in the Chair that he has noticed certain weaknesses in the candidate attendees (like a lack of real expertise or objectivity). He will advocate that their invitations be offered to others, all of whom he is sure will vote with him, promising they will be flawless meeting members.

A skilled meeting-goer-toer knows that lying and deceiving and other Machiavellian characteristics should be expected in the makeup of fellow attendees, even though such character defects might ordinarily be suppressed. These flaws of character may surface only when the individual fears the meeting's outcome will be too damaging to his interests. Such less than admirable tactics surely will not constitute high standards of behavior, but they should be expected at times. Sometimes they will work.

A friend, Fuller, once served on the board of a philanthropic foundation whose Chair was the very generous principal benefactor to the organization. Unfortunately the Chair relied on an assistant whom everyone but the Chair knew was dominated by self-interest. Fuller and the rest of the conferees had to be on their guards to counter the assistant's conniving which made the Fuller clique into schemers as well, not as bad as the sinful assistant, but Machiavellian nevertheless. Of course, in Fuller's mind, he was the good guy, one merely trying to do the right things and fight evil doing.

One very able meeting-goer-toer, Vincent, with whom I served occasionally in meetings related to a particular university, was an expert at causing the early adjournment of meetings if they were not progressing to his liking. If he observed an issue going the wrong way and if it wasn't urgent, Vincent would say something like, "This meeting is running late and this topic under discussion is still not finished. I have very important things to add that I'm sure you would want to consider. Unfortunately, however, I must leave for another meeting where I can't be late because I have to lead off there with a presentation. So how about we finish discussion of this item at the next meeting?" Vincent had an excellent batting average of delaying consideration of a meeting topic and then reaching a result he favored in a later meeting.

I once served on a classified information advisory committee with a General Elliot. Elliot would use his very high security clearance level to postpone a meeting's conclusion if he did not favor it. The General would achieve his purpose like this: "We can't decide this without including some classified facts that are very important but that, unfortunately, I cannot disclose at this moment become of its high classification. Could we possibly reschedule this item for the next meeting so as to give me time to handle this security classification problem?" Or Elliot might say: "I happen to know a specialist who is needed for this topic, someone not at this meeting. That individual, whom for certain reasons I cannot name now, has very pertinent knowledge. Could we postpone further discussion until the next meeting? I believe I can then arrange for that person to come and make a presentation. I feel sure that would be very wise." And he would usually get his way.

The General obviously had his own agenda for that meeting. Most of us have, or should have, our own carefully chosen agenda for the meetings we attend. But not all. Some meetings involve just sitting and listening. We do not expect and are not expected to contribute very much. We might simply put in our two cents worth here and there. Preparing a hidden agenda for those meetings is not a factor. If, however, we know we should play an important role in a forthcoming meeting, then it is mandatory to prepare. In real estate the three most important factors for success are location, location, and location. For the active meeting-goer-toer the three most important factors for success are preparation, preparation, and preparation. Cater to this rule and the proper hidden agenda will arise automatically.

Meeting Leading: The Chair

There are two famous rules about rules: "Rules are made to be broken" and "The exception proves the rule." Though they are repeated to the point of tiresomeness some truth resides in their elderly bones, especially since, as the rule suggests, exceptions to these rules may be expected. That will be evident as we now take up the chairing of meetings.

Chair as Leader

The chairman or chairwoman or chairperson or simply the Chair[3] of a meeting is usually the most important individual present. The Chair is likely to be the one who calls the meeting, best

---

[3] Chairper*son* and chairwo*man* obviously still contain a masculine root and bias. (We never hear of "perdaughter.") The word "chair" alone, because it is minimally sex-suggestive (overlooking the particular piece of furniture called a love seat, of course) should be preferred. Having chosen "Chair" we capitalize it.

understands why it is being called, chooses the attendees, and is most qualified to lead the meeting. The Chair usually controls—or at least influences greatly—the meeting's progress by steering the meeting along to it's outcome. Overall, then, the Chair has the best chance to bring about the meeting's success. At the same time the Chair also possesses the greatest opportunity to mess up a meeting. An incompetent or unprepared Chair can easily undermine the focus and trend of meeting discussions. Worse, a Chair's actions or inactions can cause the mandatory calling of several meetings to follow to rectify the damage created in the first badly chaired meeting. Surely then we have to understand chairing.

First we must note an exception to the importance of the Chair; some meetings may not even have a Chair and may not need one. Several individuals with a common interest may simply decide to gather and exchange thoughts with no specific leader, although one may emerge because of the meeting.

A large meeting may be held to distribute information from experts with no more than an introduction needed. The success of that meeting would not be affected meaningfully by anyone other than the speakers. We will not be interested in such exceptions; our concern here will be entirely with influential Chairs.

The characteristics of a successful Chair are not very different from the embodiments of a successful manager. The Chair must have leadership skills, and as some people have no leadership qualities so it follows that there will be bad Chairs. When this occurs it is often because criteria other than leadership qualities determine the choice of the Chair. For instance, a wealthy family's charitable foundation meetings were chaired by the senior member of the family, who was handicapped by growing senility. The other family members were hesitant to depose "grandpa," especially as the next in line to be Chair was a known alcoholic.

Mrs. Morris, the chief executive officer of a large corporation, appeared successful in running the business founded by her late husband. Mrs. Morris certainly was a tough hands-on executive. But as Chair of the board of directors her negative personality characteristics stood out. She could be narcissistic, rude, and disinterested in the views of others. It was unlikely that Morris could be successful in business with such personality shortcomings and she finally was ousted when her negative character traits became clear. However because most board members had been chosen by Morris and were well compensated, they were slow to remove her. They mistook her less than admirable characteristics for directness and forcefulness and could be forgiven for not readily perceiving and correcting this situation. Indeed, for a substantial period they actually rated her highly as a Chair. Egotism sometimes can be mistaken for self-confidence, a trait every leader needs. Similarly, rudeness can be temporarily misjudged for focus—sticking to the point firmly and quickly dismissing side issues—commonly regarded as plus in an executive.

Chair as Chameleon

Good Chairs can get things done when people are involved—a knack not everyone possesses. Excellent Chairs exhibit skill and understanding about people as well as expertise in the topics of the meeting. They are objective, considerate, and ethical. When everyone present sees evidence of these characteristics, confidence in the Chair is high and the meeting is likely to be successful. A Chair admired by the meeting participants typically presses them to come to the meeting prepared to contribute and usually that is what they do. The Chair will judge the participants' performances in the meeting while those attendees will judge the Chair. This mutual respect is critical in determining the effectiveness of the meeting.

Chairs have to possess multiple personalities and be chameleon-like if they are to lead the vast variety of meeting types with authority and finesse. Even when the chairing of a meeting is accomplished excellently, a gathering may seem to suffer from a lack of chairmanship. A Chair may allow a meeting, for example, to appear uncontrolled with everyone speaking at once, doing this to let all conferees get things off their chests and feel they have been heard. The Chair at other times will not allow an attendee to go on endlessly about a topic when the meeting should be moving along. That attendee may resent being directed by the Chair to terminate his presentation. The Chair must be capable of quickly comparing the risk of a negative with the potential gain—in this case offending one participant but allowing several others the opportunity to speak before the meeting must adjourn.

Some Chairs are top grade because they are able and willing to be mysterious when necessary; they may manipulate the attendees and plot the reaching of the meeting's conclusions. Chairs may appear sometimes to be self-centered, impatient, dogmatic, and even unfriendly; and this is bound to be the assessment of those attendees who do not approve of the way the meeting is going and with the final conclusions that seem to be emerging. The meeting's members will usually want a cheerful Chair. Yet, if a meeting is required to handle an unpleasant subject, the situation might call for a Chair with a grouchy disposition. Sometimes the Chair's ire is needed to ensure everyone's immediate concentration on the seriousness of the meeting's subject matter. All in all, a champion Chair is able to mix smiles with frowns, to be annoying when interrupting attendees' remarks then expressing sympathy and understanding a moment later. Compliments and reproaches, approvals and disapprovals, brusqueness and patience—all will be required from the Chair and will share in setting the meeting's mood.

Debate Referee

In the next chapter, we shall note that debating occupies a substantial fraction of most meetings as the attendees work out their differing or competitive views. Often the Chair becomes a referee. If you are a Chair in that situation here are some pointers:

◇ Press to reach clarity about the differences in viewpoints or claimed facts.

◇ See that the opposing disputants share arguing time fairly.

◇ Focus the debate into specific differences and do not allow expansions into vague, minor, or irrelevant issues.

◇ Surface and describe areas of agreement.

◇ Seek shifts in positions that will bring opposing stands towards agreement.

◇ If there is a right and a wrong side to the debate, steer the debate towards the right.

◇ Originate a position of your own that incorporates the best parts of the opposing positions.

◇ Force termination of debates getting nowhere.

Women as Chairs

In meetings in which the majority of attendees are men, a woman acting as Chair will suffer handicaps a man will not. Of course the whole of gender phenomena in meeting-going-toing is an important, complex, and multidimensional subject. We therefore devote a separate chapter to it later. At this point it is in order merely to list a few key points about gender bias as it affects a woman's success in chairing.

Until recent years, it has been almost impossible for women to rise to CEO status in large public corporations, or to attain high government positions, or to occupy leadership posts in academics, medicine, and law. In the past it also was uncommon for a lady to be the Chair of a meeting. Exceptions have included women succeeding (often only temporarily) their deceased husbands, or women who founded cosmetics or clothing fashion companies, or women on boards of directors of symphonies, operas, art museums, and other not-for-profit and philanthropy organizations, and of course, the numerous women's organizations.

Today, things on the gender bias front are substantially improved. Most men are capable of accepting that the best-chosen individual, male or female, should be made the Chair of a meeting. But not all men are that advanced and though the bias is not as strong as it used to be the bias remains. The resulting effects are similar to evidences of prejudice when it appears in other aspects of life. Thus, when the woman Chair is forceful in leading the meeting she may be regarded by both the male and female attendees as trying too hard to be "like a man," and she ends up being rated overly aggressive and bossy. If she is gentler than a male Chair in cutting off needless discussion or in expressing her views, or if she leads the meeting mildly, she may be thought overly soft, "just like a woman."

Women attendees will be just as watchful and critical of the female Chair as the males but for different reasons. If a woman Chair is very good looking, and especially if she is young and confident, these traits will be noticed and judged by both male and female attendees, be the latter equally beautiful or ugly. Whatever the reason, a lady Chair will sense the bias in the others' judgments of her and her awareness of this prejudice will be with her as she makes her every move, chooses her spoken words, and reacts to what anyone else at the meeting says or does. That constitutes a handicap.

Prejudice is a factor in the choice of the Chair of a meeting just as it is in choosing a dean of a university, or the head of a clinic, or an executive of a corporation. It is a bad idea to pretend prejudice does not exist, and the best advice is to acknowledge the prejudice and do your job, as Chair or attendee, male or female, as well as you can despite it. Try hard to rise above the bias. If you do it will limit the negatives greatly.

Attendee Seating

The seating arrangement for a meeting rarely gets the attention it deserves. Who sits where affects the progress of the meeting. A Chair must consider two things when drawing up a seating plan.

One is a mechanical matter of geometry and physics. If you are the Chair, you should seat attendees where they can best hear, see, and speak. In particular, locate yourself where everyone can easily see and hear you. If you are using a long rectangular table you are best situated in the middle of one side rather than placing yourself at one end. Consider where the screen should be set up and where the presenter should best stand. Think especially about the location of those participants most likely to be involved in discussions.

Ideally, you will know which attendees are very soft-spoken and require your encouragement to contribute and which attendees are hard of hearing (but choose not to wear hearing aids). Place them as best you can. If the meeting table is very large it should be equipped with microphones.

There are so many overlapping seating considerations that you may not have enough time to consider all of them fully, however, you must always give seating at least a bit of attention. Do not overlook it entirely as Chairs often do; total neglect will affect the meeting adversely enough to make you realize the wisdom of a seating plan.

If you have gone to enough trouble in planning seating that you can expect to reap some benefits, take seating one little step further. Unless the meeting is very small, it will be difficult, as the attendees assemble, for you to ad-lib directions to all of them as to where to sit. So consider setting out place cards.

The second thing a Chair must consider when drawing up a seating plan are its psychological aspects. The seating of the attendees sends out signals as to the relative status of the participants to each other, to the Chair, and perhaps to some big-shot meeting attendee as well. Egos may be involved and feelings can be bruised. I remember that Fowler, a true professional meeting-goer-toer, was exceptional. She was never bothered by where she was placed in any meeting she attended. As long as she could see, hear, and be heard she didn't interpret where she was seated as a reflection of her personal status. She did not care how others might view her or their locations. Perhaps because of her calm confidence Fowler was often placed opposite the "highest-status" attendee. There she could most conveniently engage in give and take with that VIP. Others would naturally notice that and would assume Fowler had been rated as the most knowledgeable and interesting partner for face-to-face interchange with that prominent person.

Where Should You Sit?

If neither the Chair nor anyone else sets the seating for the meeting, then attendees will sit down anywhere at random, except, regrettably, for those meeting-goer-toers who will rush to situate themselves so as to attain some perceived advantage. How should you act when there is no clear indication of where you should sit when you arrive at a meeting? First, you should try to locate a seat where you can see and hear well. It is acceptable to seek a spot next to or facing that individual with whom you can most easily exchange valuable insights about the meeting's objectives. Being of the highest character, ethics, and manners you will naturally not attempt to sit where you do not belong. For instance if you are clearly not the key participant in reaching the main decisions of the meeting, you should reconsider plunking yourself down next to the Chair or the person who *is* of key importance.

Andersen, a lady friend who was temporarily CEO of a company her late husband had founded, once told me a story. She was chairing a meeting of the company's board of directors and a luncheon was to follow for the directors plus their guest, a nationally prominent and extremely wealthy gentleman who had come to make an offer to buy the company. Andersen had set out placecards for the lunch, carefully choosing the locations of the directors in relation to her and to the VIP guest.

During a break in the board meeting before the start of the lunch, Andersen looked in at the dining room to check that everything was in place. She was surprised to spot one of her directors scurrying away from the table. Sure enough, when Andersen checked, she found he had moved his place card so as to be next to the big-wheel visitor. Of course, she quickly demoted the nervy guy to a location at the table as far away as possible. Andersen stayed in the dining room, greeted the special visitor, and seated him on her right. She then enjoyed observing the culprit going to the guest's other side expecting to see his name there but then having to search for his place. By his act that attendee permanently compromised his position with Andersen; the damage he did to his standing with her was far greater than any positive he could have gained by his misconduct as he sought improperly to improve his location at that luncheon.

Bad Chairing

Competent Chairing can be more easily defined by looking at examples of incompetent Chairing. If you avoid the bad practices of some Chairs, you will almost automatically be a Chair deserving respect. Here are some don'ts:

◇ If you are asked to Chair a meeting that has been organized by others, don't be flattered into accepting by being told you are highly respected as a Chair because you are liked personally or are so objective or skillful at running a meeting. Don't say yes unless you have an adequate knowledge of the subject matter, understand why the meeting should be held, comprehend what the meeting is expected to accomplish, know who the attendees will be, and are aware of what opposing views may be pressed by the attendees. Finally, make sure you have considered what conflicts of interest you may have or be accused of having. Incompetence will beat out objectivity and any other favorable quality you may possess when it comes to determining how you will fare as a Chair.

◇ If you are the person with the authority and responsibility for calling a meeting, don't call it unless, after reasonable consideration of the matter, you are convinced the meeting is necessary.

◇ Don't invite attendees to the meeting who are not essential to effective pursuing of the agenda. Don't invite people to attend just because they want to, or because they have been suggested by others but are in your opinion deficient, or those who are recommended as "possibly useful and probably harmless."

◇ Don't include those whom you've already noticed create problems in meetings because of their personalities.

◇ Don't invite anyone with an axe to grind unless it is important his or her views be heard.

◇ Never invite someone because he or she is a relative of yours and needs the experience.

◇ Don't call a meeting to feed your ego or anyone else's.

◇ Never call a meeting no matter how important it may appear it be held unless you have the time to prepare yourself properly, including adequate consideration of the agenda, the selection of attendees, and the problem areas for meeting discussion and debate. If you typically can't find the time to prepare for meetings you call then you should stop calling so many meetings.

◇ Cancel a planned meeting if you cannot decide what issues the meeting should address. If no such issues appear to exist, be clear as to why the meeting must be called anyway before you invite anyone to come.

◇ Don't schedule a meeting for one hour if it will really require three.

◇ Don't allow meetings to run way overtime.

◇ Contact those attendees whose contributions you think are key ahead of the meeting and urge them to prepare.

◇ Don't schedule a meeting at a time and place where terrible traffic problems will cause attendees to arrive either early or late.

◇ Identify ahead of time those issues in the meeting where as Chair you will have to lead, cajole, challenge, referee, stimulate, or censure to obtain the results the meeting should seek.

◇ Don't fail to compliment a member who has made an extraordinarily good presentation.

◇ Be ready to handle late arrivers and other problem attendees who you suspect may behave unacceptably during the meeting.

◇ Don't act like the King or Queen of a sixteenth century kingdom. Don't be obnoxiously haughty and dogmatic.

◇ Don't talk incessantly just because as Chair you may be able to get away with it.

◇ Don't call stupid attendees "stupid" in front of all the others every time they say something stupid. Find some other way to handle the situation or you may become known as a Stupid Chair.

◇ Contemplate the results of each meeting you Chair afterwards so as to note what went well and what was disappointing, especially as to your own performance as Chair.

◇ Don't cancel a meeting and fail to inform all attendees early enough to prevent their leaving for it.

Presenters, Debaters, and Commentators

At any moment in a meeting someone is likely to be speaking. The talk may comprise a quick sentence, the naming of a person or a place, a short question, or just a yes or no response. Anything longer, such as a considerable conveyance of information or reasoning, or a talk that has required substantial effort for its preparation and delivery, should be considered a presentation. Presentations use up a big fraction of the time spent in a typical meeting and together with the associated discussion constitute the essence of the meeting. Thus a skilled meeting-goer-toer's qualifications must include being a good presenter, however, many conferees' presentations are abysmal. Why do so many presentations fail to inform attendees clearly and efficiently of facts, analyses, ideas, and recommendations? What characterizes a top presenter? How can you become one?

Misused Equipment

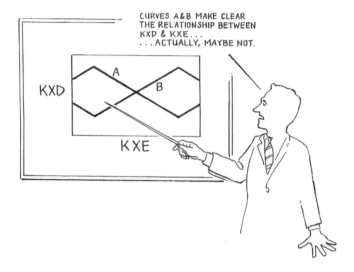

There are many technical gadgets that allow information to be easily given out at meetings. Data and lines of thought can be incorporated into readily produced visuals. Words, numbers, pictures, diagrams, graphs, pie charts, and complex patterns can be displayed with high visibility and in color. Microphones and speakers make it possible that even in large meetings every attendee will hear every syllable presenters utter. Surprisingly many presenters fail to employ these aids competently.

Some otherwise skilled presenters are clumsy in the use of a mike; for instance a tall person following a shorter individual onto the podium will often neglect to raise the microphone. Instead he leans way over into the low microphone and assumes a painful-looking bent position for the delivery of his entire remarks. Others will step up to the mike, say a few words, then move away to point to the screen's display and start a back and forth walk while talking, pacing being a conspicuous part of their speaking pattern. If they must walk as they talk, they should use a readily available clip-on microphone. Some meeting-goer-toers will carefully prepare the content of their presentations, devotedly employing all their professional expertise as they do so, and then they will amateurishly flunk out in their employment of the right acoustic aids.

Another sign of a poor presenter is one who has placed too

much information on his chart. Modern computer programs allows these presenters to generously and unforgivably overload—delirious with the quantity of data now available to them, these presenters want to display it all. They are oblivious to the fact that their viewers cannot focus on, sort out, and assimilate everything that has been forced onto the screen. These presenters favor graphs with too many curves and hieroglyphs; the pies on their charts have too many cuts with hard-to-read multiple-word names for each segment. They err further by showing charts with the letters and numbers far too small for anyone in the meeting to read. These speakers show a further lack of understanding of their audience by placing unnecessary titles at the top of their display in big letters that hog the most visible upper half of their charts.

An example is a presentation made recently at a meeting I attended. It was given by Carson, a manager heading a unit of one division of a parent corporation, each of these three organizational levels being named with large letters, one below the other, using up the upper portion of each of his charts. Carson was presenting his budget for the year ahead with his listeners interested mainly in the lowest part of the display where all the key numbers appeared. He stood near his screen that was set at a low height at the end of a long table. Almost all attendees had someone else's body between their eyes and the screen. Most of us could clearly see only the highest third of each chart. It was monopolized by titles. We managed occasional glimpses of the interesting lower part by constantly shifting our positions as we sought to see around some other participant's head.

How could Carson not have realized that we did not need to be reminded of the name of the company on each chart? The numbers we really wanted to see were presented in irritatingly small sizing. Only Carson and those seated near him could hope to view the budget total at the very bottom of the chart. A competent presenter would have arranged to get the screen placed higher and he would have left off entirely the organization's names, which would have enabled the really useful information to be visible and readable.

Carson did not reach the pinnacle of visual presentation ineptness that day. That peak is attained regularly by those presenters who inadvertently place themselves between the projector and the screen. As they speak, facing the listeners, the intense light beaming from the projector hits their eyes and casts a massive shadow of the speaker's head on the screen. That obstructs the complex diagrams about which they are speaking. I saw this absurd act performed once by a Dr. Hayes, an internationally prominent professor. As I watched him I knew that it wasn't his lone performance; he'd probably taken years to refine the art. As he stood in the projector's light stream, squinting painfully, I heard him mutter "that damn light!" all the while choosing to remain in the dazzling glare rather than moving sideways about two feet.

On that occasion Professor Hayes also employed three colors to distinguish three different curves that were overlapping on his most important chart. The three colors were (1) orange, (2) a slightly lighter shade of orange, and (3) a tiny bit slightly darker orange. As he spoke about each separate curve he referred to these virtually identical orange colors (as seen by his audience) as red, orange, and yellow. We never could be clear as to which of the three curves he was referring to at any moment.

Where's That Pointer?

Then there is the nutty "Where's the pointer?" game played by certain mediocre presenters. They know ahead of time that they will want to point to items on the display screen or on their flip charts as they make their presentations. Nonetheless they are negligent in arranging ready access to a pointer when needed. Logically they should want to know where that good old wooden slim stick pointer or the new laser beam emitter is located before they get up to talk. Instead, they do nothing until the moment when they need to point. Then they start searching for the pointer. All the attendees immediately try to help. Everyone gets into the game of peering everywhere about the room for the pointer while neither the speaker nor his audience is involved in the subject matter of the meeting.

"Like Y'Know"

Any presentation can be destroyed by the painful speaking habits of the presenter. Misdeeds in using the English language include woeful errors in grammar, silly speech idiosyncrasies, overuse of trite expressions, undignified mispronunciations, and atrocious enunciation in general. Consider some examples.

It is common to hear people severely handicapped by limited vocabularies encumber their comments with speech fragments such as, "y' know," "like," and "like, y' know." When aptly employed these expressions can impart meanings. If, for instance, you want to recognize that your listeners already know a particular thing, something you nevertheless have good reason to mention anyway, then the words "you know" can make sense. Contrast this with carelessly plopping a meaningless "y' know" between every two words of every sentence. This can be so irritating to the listeners that it quickly destroys their respect for the speaker. By insistently uttering the wearisome syllabic duo, "y'know," speakers disclose they cannot find real words to express their thoughts. When that becomes clear to the listeners, they will wish the speakers wouldn't try and would just shut up instead. The thoughts the speakers are trying to convey end up being rated by the audience as far less important than they might deserve to be. The messages may be rejected in their entirety.

I for Me

Most of us commit occasional errors in grammar when carrying on a conversation. Even when noticed such faults usually are forgiven by the listener. Should the grammar flaw be bad enough to render the meaning unclear, the speaker may be asked to repeat what was said, a tolerable deviation from perfection in the presentation. But some errors, particularly when the same ones are made repeatedly during a meeting offering, can ruin it.

As an example, an epidemic of a particular grammatical error is spreading in the U.S. It is saying "and I" instead of the correct "and me." "They met my wife *and I* at the airport." "The contest was won by Alan *and I*." "He knew Bill *and I*." The devil's rule in this agonizing misuse of the language is that *"and me"* (never *"and I"*) must always follow when the *"I"* speaker tells of sharing with someone, as in "He helped Mary and me" or "They asked John and me to come." The grammatical abomination *"and I"* is heard daily in the speech of mature, otherwise seemingly sophisticated people. I heard it recently performed repetitively by a U.S. senator.

I recently went to a meeting honoring a new Nobel Laureate. In his remarks he misused numerous *"and Is"* as he described how well Sweden took care of "my wife *and I*" when he went there to receive his award. Apparently to him *"and I"* sounds more correct than *"and me,"* no matter what words precede it. He would never say "He drove I," yet he was happy with offering. "He drove my wife and I." I concluded that he is a crude person, or he could not bear to speak the language so sloppily. I would take his advice seriously on a physics issue, but not on any other subject.

Uh, Uh, Uh

A second speaking sin reaches higher rungs on the bothersomeness ladder. If you pause often in the middle of sentences while speaking—as you seek the right word or phrase, or while trying to recall a name or date, or when unclear how best to express the thought on your mind—it is not necessarily a problem. The listener readily overlooks such pauses and they can even add dramatic touches to spoken phrases. Bill Clinton was expert in exploiting "the pause." Of course, he didn't need long rests before coming up with the words he wanted to use. Most people are not so articulate, so their pauses are longer and more frequent. Still they are not sources of discomfort for the listeners. Government and business leaders, prominent authors, professors, actors, even professional television interviewers regularly mix long and short pauses with their predicates, adjectives, and prepositions as they talk. We listen to them quite happily.

What is vastly different, definitely noticed and not forgiven, is to fill each pause with the very audible syllable "uh," as in: "I uh need uh to explain what I uh mean by the uh uh." This string of "uhs" is a deplorable speaking defect. Almost everyone does it to some extent. (Even one of the greatest extemporaneous speakers of our time, Defense Secretary Donald Rumsfeld, does it a bit.) Too many do it to an absurd degree. When you next watch TV news or interviews in which the speakers are not reading a prompter but are just talking, listen for the uhs. You will find they are expelled generously, add nothing, and in high quantities are extremely irksome.

What is this uh thing, anyway? It is not a word, yet its devotees seem to regard it as a necessary unit of speech. What do they think the uttered "uh" adds to their conversation? Must some sound emanate from the larynx regularly so the listener will know the speaker is still there and alive? Why isn't a silent pause better?

Most uh abusers settle for a short uh sound, but other uhers produce long, sustained uhs. Maybe they are inspired by the great operatic tenors who thrill audiences with the strong and beautiful notes they can hold forever without running out of breath. The speakers who fall into such an odious pattern of speech intersperse the words of their spoken language with "mega-uhs," enthusiastic, lengthy, vibrato-loaded concert quality emissions.

Like sound sleepers who are certain they never snore, being asleep at the time, so never hearing it, most uh-ers do not realize how uh-ish they are. If their best friends should mention it, the uhers (like alcoholics) will deny and resent it. If you're not an uher, your real words, even when separated by soundless pauses, will be listened to by your audience. But that same audience will be most unappreciative if they are forced to endure barrages of uhs between your words. Listen critically to your speaking voice and if you discover you are a prolific uh-er set out to curb this ugly negative. It's like stopping smoking. No matter how difficult it may be to quit, you must because otherwise your habit will kill you, and you should quit uh-ing because otherwise it will murder your presentations.

Here's how to quit. First, buy a cheap audio recording and playback device. Then, pick up a memo or report you need to read anyway and quickly scan two or three paragraphs. Next, turn away and tell the recorder, in your own words, the substance of what you just read. Do this a few times a day for a week or two. Then play it all back and listen—you will be surprised how many uhs you will hear. On the first recording you'll keep the quantity of uhs down and your pauses will be longer than normal because you know that you are being tested. But soon you'll settle into your regular uh-ing pattern. Keep doing this little exercise and you will steadily develop the discipline that enables cutting out the nasty uhs. You will still employ pauses during your speech because you will still need to hesitate as you choose your next words. But you will pause silently; it will be without the horrid accompaniment of uhs.

Acronyms and Abbreviations

Presenters can lose their audiences in other ways, and tossing off acronyms and abbreviations carelessly is one of them. When experts communicate with each other such codes can be useful, often essential for reasonable efficiency. The names of weapons systems, economic measures, accounting symbols, bacteria, government organizations, genes, computer software, plants, bugs, and others typically consist of several words or poly syllables, so numerous are the variations and the need for quickly distinguishing terms one from another during discussions. This naturally makes acronyms and abbreviations sensible when speaking to some audiences.

Thus a presenter will use the acronym ICBM for Intercontinental Ballistic Missile during a meeting with defense system engineers. Acronyms such as USA, the UN, IRS, NATO, and CEO are universally understood. It's another thing, however, to say things like "the SFCF is superior to the RRE in its DNX rating on the 2F VRA" to an audience that doesn't understand any of the acronyms used. The attendees are puzzled by the presenter's recital of mysterious fragments of the alphabet, and a total failure of communication and understanding results.

Meeting speakers who use acronyms that do not register with their listeners disclose a lack of the most basic talent a good communicator must possess, the ability to put oneself in the position of the listener. Presenters with such shortcomings will exhibit their lack of common communication sense in many other ways when they seek to convey information. They are prone to inadvertently using phrases with more than one possible meaning without realizing that the listener may take the wrong meaning. They will insert trivial and boring details the audience is disinterested in and that will add nothing to the listeners' understanding. Unneeded elaborations will turn meeting members off and allow them to start thinking of other things during the presentation. Moreover, basic communication skill shortages often accompany an inability to recognize when enough is enough. Along with parading their acronyms and poor choice of detail and words, these presenters will carry on too long. Finally, a lack of humor often goes with a shortage of speaking skills, and is further evidence of the presenters inability to sense how others think. When a humor-challenged speaker tries to employ wit the result is usually sad rather than funny.

Speaking English

An accent can either enhance or impair a presentation. Maurice Chevalier's French accent surely aided his charming of American audiences. For some, Kissinger's Teutonic vocal touches subtly support his deserved image of expertise in international affairs. In meetings it is only necessary that the presenter, whether with an accent or not, be easily understood. Of course, some accents (from Brooklyn, rural Southern states, Russia, sometimes New York, Texas, and Boston) can generate negatives with prejudiced listeners even when the words are readily understood. Fortunately, if the meaning of the speaker is clear, pertinent, and worthy of serious attention by the listeners, an accent will not penalize a presentation's success.

Speakers with poor enunciation, however, force their audiences to hold to extremely high levels of focused attention in order to understand the presenter's words. These speakers will not be listened to intently for long. News anchors on TV are selected for their ability to speak words correctly and clearly. You don't have to be that good to perform well in your meetings. But your departures from perfection should not be huge either. Even the best speaker can occasionally use "duh" for "the" and leave off the "g" in "ing;" but this must be kept to a minimum—the word "to" should not be sounded as "tuh" as in "it's time tuh go to duh meetin'." Sometimes it's nice to hear "yes" in place of "yeah." Avoid the pitiful and pervasive "jaw" virus that infects the speech of some, as in "couldjaw" for "could you," "didjaw," for "did you," "wouldjaw," for "would you." And finally, don't look down on those famous residents of certain parts of London who speak with a so-called Cockney accent, and don't sound the "h" when pronouncing a word beginning with "h." At least we should recognize a kinship with those mispronouncers when we say "Iyav" when we should say "I have," as in "Iyav tah go" in place of "I have to go."

I am not urging meeting presenters to attempt to speak English the way Lord Lawrence Olivier did. It would, however, cause speakers at meetings to earn greater respect and more serious consideration of the points they seek to make if they could develop one particularly good speech habit. This is to end each word's final consonant before starting the next word. As an example, try to say the previous sentence aloud using this rule and you'll sound positively British (incidentally, not Bridish, as we Americans say it).

Speech Affectations

I have a friend, Sally, who is a truly professional meeting-goer-toer. Yet Sally's presentations and even her casual conversations are marred by her insistence on placing "point in" ahead of the word "time." Sally uses "at that point in time" rather than "at that time." The word "time" comes up frequently in meetings because so much of the conversation requires identifying when an incident occurred. Sally never says "now." She belabors it to "at this point in time." Sally must have picked up the term "point in time" from Einstein, who had an excuse to use it. Albert had need in some of his equations to locate a point by four dimensions, three in space and one in time, the whole region being measured in "space-time." This probably has some value when working with the theory of relativity but doubtless has nothing whatever to do with Sally's observations. "At that point in time" is an affectation. Affected speech is not good speech and impairs meeting presentations.

Many in the State Department and the Pentagon engage in myriads of fads and airs that lower the quality of their presentations. The phrase "In terms of," for instance, is becoming more and more popular. Ask a question and the government expert will open with "In terms of that question" or "In terms of the budget . . ." or "In terms of planning . . ." or "In terms of an answer . . ." Since "In terms of" means nothing and says less, we can only hope this ponderous speech pattern will disappear—the sooner the better.

A phrase that can be similarly aggravating when misused over and over is "In a manner of speaking." Ask whether the project will be on time and the answer is "Yes—in a manner of speaking." Ask for a comment on any subject and the rejoinder will commence with "In a manner of speaking . . ." This phrase can provide a useful warning of vagueness or incompleteness in the statement to follow, and thus have some communications value. As a rule if you employ the phrase "in a manner of speaking," it only *sounds* like you are saying something. Don't let "in a manner of speaking" become *your* manner of speaking. It's not a manner with great attractions.

Sentence openers such as "To be honest" and "in all honesty" or "To tell the truth" deliver an unintended message. They suggest that the speaker ordinarily does not tell the truth and that an exception is about to be heard. This is probably not the impression the speaker intends. Perhaps he meant to say something more like: "What I am going to state is true, even if at first it may not seem to be." Exclude the intro of "honestly, folks" and its full range of equivalents from your speaking style.

Bad speech habits are easy to acquire and hard to break. Don't fall in love with inane and negative word groups. If you discover you are overusing a phrase that merely takes up space between the good parts of your presentations, assume your comments will be clearer and more welcome to your listeners if you junk those phrases.

Debating

Debating is the most important aspect of speaking at a meeting. Put two people together for a serious discussion of something important to them—a problem or opportunity or challenge with no obvious best way to handle it—and they will almost certainly exhibit some variance in their views. If the meeting is attended by six, eight, or ten participants debating will constitute a major meeting activity. Because agenda items are often important to the personal success of the attendees, different ideas about those items will be expressed in a typical meeting; debating is the natural vehicle for resolving these differences. It is necessary that a meeting-going-toer be a good debater because so many decisions in a meeting develop through the debate process and will determine key policies, strategic priorities and which people attain responsibilities and influence. Good debaters tend to dominate the discussions and the conclusions of a meeting. They will generally get their way, right or wrong, because of their debating skills. If you wish to be a successful meeting-goer-toer, you must be able to win these meeting debates.

Debaters can be divided into two classes, the naturals, and the strugglers. You are a natural if you were on the debating team in college. You are a natural if you are an attorney who handles court cases. You are a natural if you excelled in a university course in logic or if you were born with the "gift of gab." Naturals possess the basic debating talent vital to fully developed meeting-goer-toers.

But suppose that as a debater you are a struggler. Strugglers have neither an inherent debating flair nor a background of education and experience that provide them advantages in debating. How can a struggler come out on top in meeting discussions, especially when your argument is the most appropriate solution for the problem the meeting is to solve? What a shame if your point of view is the strongest but fails to get the meeting's support because you lack skill as a debater.

All meeting debaters, naturals or strugglers, should be absolutely clear in their own mind of the position they take in meetings. If you are a struggler, the most effective way to attain success in debating is solid, extensive preparation. You must lay out with care the case you plan to make well ahead of the meeting's opening. Persevere to understand the strong and weak points of your position. Seek the highest logic in the former and ways to strengthen the latter. This planning applies not only to those meetings when you will be allocated substantial time to make an uninterrupted presentation—the debates you must prepare for will most often arise informally, with sudden give and take discussion during the meeting being the pattern. That means that part of your homework is devising a way to get your arguments into the discussion whenever you get the chance.

You must anticipate your case being attacked by those who don't agree with you. What will they claim is weak or wrong about your points? How should you respond? Don't leave it to the meeting to invent your answers on the spot. Your opponents, the natural debaters, will be quick to adlib their side of the debate with pertinent, well-stated, fresh-sounding commentary tailored to the unpredictable way the debate might go. You will have to try to do that too, as best you can. But you must try to anticipate and consider how the argument might develop before you leave for the meeting.

While you plan imagine that you are on the other side; what might be the views and recommendations of your opponents in contrast to your proposals and reasoning? What will be their weak points? What specific issues do you think the principal debating will be about? Where exactly will you and your opponents differ?

As well as adopting the habit of adequate preparation, certain aspects of your debating skills need to be developed. At times your best plan in a meeting may be to take a determined stand and press quite insistently for consideration of your proposals. You may win, even against great debaters, if they are wrong and you stick it out. At other times you will be a more valuable meeting-goer-toer if you arrive ready to be flexible. You should be prepared to modify your arguments if during the debate you come to see that your opponents' views are advantageous to the overall cause. You should always be willing to negotiate because that is part of the useful employment of debating.

The Must-Win Debater

Suppose you are convinced you are right about an issue that will be argued in a coming meeting, but you lack confidence in your ability to win because you are a poor debater. Before the meeting starts approach the best debater among the attendees and try to convince her to buy your views. Seek a meeting of just the two of you where, with no audience, you will have a better chance to sell your arguments. If you're convinced your ideas really are superior, you should try to recruit a great debate partner ahead of time.

Don't try this, however, with a debater like Hansen, an individual who presented me and the other members of the board we served with distressing challenges. Unlike Hansen, the rest of us would apply ourselves to considering objectively every issue needing analysis and decision, and we would try hard to settle on the best action. Hansen, in contrast, would turn every discussion into a debate. He was an extremely clever and competitive debater and wanted every meeting to consist of debates he would win. When it seemed to the rest of us that we had clearly reached the proper conclusion, Hansen would disagree. He would find some additional angle to bring up and develop and use it to suggest we were wrong. He would take any statement we might make and seek to prove it was not necessarily correct in every little respect. He would challenge some bit of data we might cite and demand proof. He would skillfully employ tricks of language to intrigue us with his performance and get our minds off the subject.

If Hansen had acted this way only occasionally and briefly we might have looked forward to his contributions because his skill in expressing himself was extremely entertaining. Hansen was so set on winning, however, that when he saw he had no chance to do so he would invent facts that we all knew were incorrect. But he could not accept being found wrong about anything. He would keep on arguing, using up valuable meeting time and exhausting the patience of all of us.

If you run into a Hansen, don't try to get him on your side ahead of the meeting, even if you are dead sure you are right and only need help in convincing others. A Hansen is not interested in being right. He simply wants to win.

Unnecessary Commentating

Lastly we will discuss a meeting behavior that is less a matter of competence than one of bad habits. During any meeting it is likely that a substantial fraction of what is said by the attendees does not really need saying. Talk is not helpful unless it advances the meeting's progress, and some windy commentaries need not be started. A comment shouldn't be made if it misinforms, offends, takes up valuable time, and delays useful discussion. Experienced meeting-goer-toers expect in a typical conference to have to put up with much annoying commentating by others. Accordingly, they seek to limit any superfluous contributions to the meeting. As participants, they will try to avoid making egregious errors such as these:

⋄ Talking when you don't know what you're talking about.

⋄ Repeating in detail what others have already said, and worse, getting it wrong.

⋄ Clarifying a point that needs no clarification because it is already clear to everyone.

⋄ Agreeing with something said by others but going far beyond saying "I agree."

⋄ Expressing disagreement with something said by others which they did not say and you alone misunderstood.

⋄ Introducing personal experiences to provide still another example when others have already presented adequate examples and the point has been well made.

⋄ Making "yes-man" comments every time the boss or some other very influential attendee makes a statement.

⋄ Bringing up a minor issue that relates only slightly if at all to the matter under consideration.

⋄ Offering another alternative when the decision has been made and the long meeting is adjourning.

⋄ Asking a question that has already been answered, showing you have not understood the previous discussion.

⋄ Saying things that, if you would only have thought a bit before opening your mouth, you would have realized you should not have said.

⋄ Talking just to hear yourself talk.

5

Your Meeting Personality

Your success in a meeting is determined as much by your personality as by your expertise in the topics covered. By personality we mean the way you treat others, speak, listen, smile, or frown—your poise, patience, friendliness. Your intensity of feeling, tolerance, expression or suppression of animosity or jealousy, your attitudes, even the way you dress are all part of your personality.

The culture of a meeting is not determined by its agenda. It is the people who attend the meeting that set the accepted behavior pattern, and they may come from various walks of life. In Japan it can be considered rude to get right into the business of a meeting immediately after being seated. Before work begins a short period of small talk and some sips of tea are expected—meeting foreplay. What constitutes good meeting manners has to be defined separately for gatherings of mayors, football coaches, accountants, politicians, academics, CEOs, or musicians. The way a group of scientists act towards each other in a meeting is likely to differ from the conduct of business executives assembled to discuss a deal. Still, some aspects of approved behavior will be the same for all groups. Remember, some imperfections in the personalities of individual meeting-goer-toers should remain hidden no matter what kind of meeting they attend!

Cultural differences can mean that preferred manners in one nation would feel like a slight in another, and this contradiction is reflected in various rules of civil behavior. "Treat others as you would like to be treated" seems both a high-minded and a practical rule. Also sounding sensible and useful is "When in Rome do as the Romans do." But Romans may regularly treat others differently from how Romans would like themselves to be treated. Other folks may not choose anything like the treatment you or I would like to receive ourselves.

Social behavior is subjective: if you come into a meeting with messy hair, you could be considered a slob or you could look just right if the other attendee's hairdos disclose the same disinterest in barbers and soap. Remember: to optimize your chances of success in a meeting abide by the code of behavior of the other attendees be it manners, speaking habits, or attire. The one exception to this is any situation where it might be important for you to make the point that you are different from the others. In such a situation you may succeed or fail depending in great part on how you look and how you react to the other attendees. Whether for good or ill, whether out of deliberately planned strategy, or resulting by accident or pure ignorance, your conduct will affect the way your proposals and your performance will be perceived.

The Grade A Personality

It requires much more than being perceived as "nice" for your meeting personality to be rated excellent; overly anxious politeness may even be regarded as an affectation. What some may see as intolerable brusqueness may meet with favor by others who take it as evidence of firmness of character or straight-forwardness or leadership strength, all qualities deserving admiration. An extreme rule for participants at some meetings may be simply to hurry and get the job done—to discuss, decide, and move on; a concern for "manners" might be judged by this "efficiency" crowd as irrelevant to the task at hand. In some corporation meetings, possessing a highly acceptable personality might equate to copying the characteristics of the CEO whether or not those manifestations are rated high by all.

So, what constitutes a desirable meeting personality and what is proper meeting conduct? We should not expect simple definitions because meetings are, after all, microcosms of life, of people acting and reacting with one another. Meetings are arenas where people engage in being human. In the process they may provide each other, off and on, with support or antagonism, at varying times agreeing, differing, loving, hating, competing, and cooperating. All persons' personalities are complex. The many qualities making up an individual's nature at any given time may show themselves or be hidden. Different components of one's makeup will dominate then fade away, especially as seen by others. An attendee's behavior in a meeting can change in seconds as a result of how a meeting topic develops or in response to someone else's attitude. Despite the complexity and challenge of the subject, some basics stand out and deserve our notice.

Tension: The Personality Destroyer

There is no excuse for your not exhibiting an attractive meeting personality if the meeting proceeds smoothly and as planned. Imagine that you are on the agenda to make a presentation, and you perform perfectly. You choose and present the right material and score high in the question and answer session because you are expert in your subject. Your boss is there and is impressed, your associates treat you with respect. The rest of the agenda interests you and the debating that takes place is performed by competent and gentle fellow attendees. The meeting is a great success for you, your boss, and all participants. You leave with a sense of accomplishment and security. You look forward to the next meeting with relish.

If this is your typical meeting experience, then you should count yourself lucky. You obviously have the privilege of working with a group of people who get along well. Your boss is capable and considerate and you are appreciated by all. Yours is not a life of hectic meeting tension. You should think twice about changing jobs.

But now consider the other extreme. Suppose that even the contemplation of the meeting you are going to attend puts you into an unhappy and emotional state. You have to make a presentation and you expect it to go badly no matter how hard you prepare. Your boss, you have reason to believe, is considering firing you. Your presentation will be rudely interrupted by him again and again; he will be, as usual, overly critical, you feel unfairly so.

The boss won't be the only person giving you trouble. Several of the attendees are so incapable that they will fail to understand many of your best points and will surely demonstrate that with their stupid comments. Much of what they will say will infuriate you, especially the comments of a certain attendee who wants your job. He is a man who stamps with glee on all your arguments but never effectively answers them. You are concerned to the point of extreme nervousness that he will put you into a frenzy, that you will lose your cool, and you will tell him off. You know you have a bad temper and you are frightened that you will not be able to hide that in the meeting. Even if you don't go overboard in your reaction to everyone else's behavior, you are sure you will not have a decent opportunity to demonstrate your exceptional talents. You will not be seen as what you are, a very decent, mature, capable team member with a most attractive personality.

This will be a tension meeting. The stress will be more than

PRESENTATION AT A TENSION MEETING

you can put up with. You wish you didn't have to be involved in such meetings.

Tension meetings are not the typical meeting experience for most meeting-goer-toers. If it happens to you frequently, you must either adjust or you must change jobs. But suppose you believe that high-stress meetings must be expected to occur occasionally in your job, a position you really like. How can you best handle tension meetings when they do happen? Two suggestions:

1) Make a list of the worst things that could happen in the coming meeting, emphasizing those that will most likely trigger your responding out of distress, disgust, pressure, and rage.

2) List next the actions you might find yourself taking, especially the bad performance you might stoop to out of the emotional strain of the moment—the lapses of judgment you might generate—everything that you will later wish you had not done or said. Force yourself to imagine these things in detail, picture them as if they actually happened.

If you go through this listing and imagining exercise, you will find that you will hold your responses in the actual meeting to a lower temper and anguish level. You will not lose control. You will conduct yourself better.

What if this does not work? What if tension meetings appear likely to become more frequent? You then ought to look for a new job.

The Old and the Young

The personality that defines you in a meeting depends in part on your fellow attendees. Are they like you or completely different? Meetings with people used to a different meeting behavior than you are accustomed to can be difficult. As an example, we will indulge in a colossal oversimplification and exaggeration, and arbitrarily divide all meeting-goer-toers into two categories, Young and Old. The Young will be those in their twenties and thirties (and, for some, into their forties). The Old are those in their fifties (with some getting old in their forties) and on into the sixties, seventies, and beyond. Let us look at how these two age groups see each other when they must interact in meetings.

The Old see the Young as immature: lacking wisdom, experience, patience, and courtesy. The Young, they feel, are rude, unmannerly, and sassy. They are conceited and show little respect for the views of each other let alone of their elders who possess the graces and refinements they lack. Their attire makes it painful for eyes to behold them. Their awful, peculiarly narrow vocabulary and their ignorance of grammar make their speech a noisy, offensive, unclear mess of syllables that is not only difficult for ears to accept but suggests they are unable to think clearly. Their proposals are naïve and impractical and, while they believe their every idea to be a breakthrough, they actually reinvent old failures and merely add new elements of confusion.

As a result of the above the Old feel they must be especially careful, ready, and responsible when in meetings with the Young, and be diligent in preventing unsound schemes from being adopted. The Old have a duty to educate and advise, and most importantly, to provide essential leadership.

The Young see the Old as out-of-date, behind the times, too anxious to give advice, grossly overrating the value of their experience, overly conservative and cautious and unaware of the inaccuracies in their faulty memories. Furthermore, they are cranky, disrespectful of anyone ten years younger than themselves, talk too much in meetings about the past, think they have the answer to every problem, and are influential purely as a result of their years of accumulation of power rather than of genuine competence. They ought to take retirement far earlier than they are planning.

My personal friends, the Mitchells, Senior and Junior, father and son, think of each other in the ways described above. I am very close to Senior and an honorary uncle to Junior. Mitchell, Sr., now sixty-eight, created and still runs a successful company manufacturing switches and other electric parts. Junior, thirty-six, after working under his father in the family company for five years, started his own company selling air conditioning equipment.

Junior is on the board of Senior's company. Senior is on the board of Junior's company.

In great confidence, they each tell me of their dissatisfaction with each other's participation in the two board meetings. Senior most frequently complains that his son does not dress appropriately, has too many young "punks" on the board who lack experience, and does not speak properly. Junior says his father is closed-minded, and pushes ways to solve problems that worked decades ago but aren't applicable to today's greatly changed world.

There is a great deal of affection between Senior and Junior, and they would always rather help than quarrel with each other. The point is that their personalities and behaviors are different when they find themselves together in meetings than when each is in a meeting with his own age group. Their familial relationship may make them unusual, but most meetings these days include both Young and Old, and interested observers can readily observe the personality adjustments taking place as attendees of different age groups deal with each other. Making these situations even more interesting is the fact that some meeting-goer-toers low in years act Old, and some oldsters act Young. Furthermore, the negative aspects that each group loosely characterizes as true of the other often apply to members of both age groups.

The Old do have experience worth listening to most of the time and it is sensible for the Young to encourage the Old to contribute their stories. The Old, having felt both success and failure, are likely to have something valuable to say that may increase the chances of future successes and decrease the likelihood of failures. The Old are particularly skillful at sizing up people—they can sense a phony right away—and they can quickly spot unsound ideas and plans.

The Young are often creative. They are more likely to be bold, optimistic, determined, ambitious, and anxious to contribute. Their thinking is not highly handicapped by overdwelling on the possibility of failure. They are eager to accept challenges and do not believe "it can't be done." No matter how tough a task appears, most Young will take it on. They are ready and willing to learn and they usually will accept advice and assistance from the Old if properly presented.

We have discussed the generation gap as one example of a general truism: Meeting-goer-toers are more comfortable with other attendees who are like themselves. Their personalities and conducts are at their best then and that is important for successful meeting-going-toing. However, it is vital to become skilled at meeting with people who are different from oneself. Differences offer advantages in arriving at the best meeting results and the positive values of diversity should be pursued.

Confidentiality Problems

Ethics combined with good manners define acceptable conduct in meetings when comments by attendees about other people are needed. For example, a meeting's objective may be to discuss whom to promote to fill an opening, or whether a specific person should be hired, promoted, or fired. In such meetings no problems of ethics and manners will arise if attendees have been carefully selected so that all can speak their minds freely. It's different when remarks about particular individuals where not planned but suddenly seem necessary. For instance, someone asks in a meeting whether a particular job should be assigned to Mr. X and Mr. Y, who is present, is sure Mr. X would be very wrong for the role. Should he say so? Meeting-goer-toers will find situations arise when they cannot tell the other members something they know is important and pertinent. We sight examples.

Suppose an attendee brings us an issue unaware that upper management is planning to solve the matter by firing Bradley. You happen to know this, but you also know Bradley's dismissal is not ready for announcement. Maybe you cannot speak to the subject then and there for another bothersome reason, namely, that Bradley happens to be present at the meeting and is sitting right next to you.

Some confidentiality situations are clearly defined, namely those controlled by military secrecy regulations or by corporate contracts and legally based board rulings. In those instances you know exactly what to do. You simply do not disclose knowledge you possess to anyone not entitled to be a recipient of it—period! No matter how severely pressured, you unhesitatingly say that you can't and won't provide that information. You will always be alert to avoid accidental disclosures through inadvertent conversational slips. You will make certain that proper clearance is granted before you allow yourself to engage in discussion about such matters.

But big, fat gray areas abound. For instance, you may be in a budget proposal meeting where the other attendees are assuming a specific project will be approved. You, however, have just come from a higher-level management meeting where you learned that particular project was assigned a low priority by the top executives and they have decided to cancel it entirely. Do you disclose this fact at the present meeting even though the instructions given during the previous meeting was to keep everything confidential? Do you stay quiet and let the meeting end with an unrealistic number for that project in the budget preparation?

Another example: you are a member of the search committee to find a new dean at a college. The other members of the committee, you observe, are settling on your friend, Susan, an outstanding professor, as their first choice for the new dean, and they will present that to the college president for action. But Susan has told you, very confidentially, that she has almost decided—but is not yet certain and thus has pledged you to secrecy—to accept an offer at another college. Do you say something?

Again, Hogan, a speaker at a management meeting, presents key data regarding a coming decision, and you are sure that his numbers are not correct. Moreover, you have been told that Hogan is under investigation for habitually falsifying information. You have been instructed, however, not to disclose that fact because it may interfere with the investigation's successful completion. Do you leave the meeting without questioning Hogan's numbers even though, with the meeting's attendees acting in ignorance, they may reach a wrong decision?

There are some guiding principles for dealing with these confidentiality dilemmas in a meeting. Firstly you should always be well prepared for your meetings; before going to a powwow ask yourself whether any confidentiality issues may confront you there. Be imaginative and err on the side of overpreparing. If a particular situation comes do mind while you do this exercise, consider whether your response could cause you a problem. You can plan, for instance, to stay quiet, come what may. Or, when the item comes up, you can announce you have important knowledge but can't reveal it. You can try to postpone the taking up of the issue at the meeting, or you can disclose some pieces of what you know and refuse to tell more. Or you can say nothing and get up and leave the meeting suddenly, embarrassing as that might seem.

No Secrets, No Pledges

To avoid these difficult situations you should refuse to accept secrets, and never make pledges not to tell, recognizing that you may have to break confidentiality. If the boss has informed you of something she is planning but is not ready to announce, tell her you might find yourself in an impossible situation in a meeting and press her for advice as to what she would prefer you do under such circumstances. Don't worry that she will be annoyed by your question or that she will cross you off her list of close, confidential advisors. On the contrary, she probably will respect you more for showing your breadth in thinking ahead and preparing yourself.

Put the baton now in the other hand—never tell people secrets and ask they be kept. Recognize that your secret's recipient will be put in a very awkward position if he is in a meeting where the subject of your secret is raised. In such a stressful situation pressure can build on your confidant, leading to unplanned and penalizing disclosures. It is human nature that the confidentiality you seek may be broken. Recall the Daniel Ellsburg case. He was made famous by his decision, as a matter of his sincere conscience, to disclose classified Pentagon papers that he believed showed the nation's leadership had engaged in deception in getting into and carrying out the Vietnam War. He didn't keep the secrets.

VIPs in Meetings

When discussing meeting manners, a special category deserves attention. This is a meeting of dignitaries. A meeting peopled by big shots will differ from a normal meeting in how the meeting has come about, what its agenda is, how it is chaired, how the attendees act, and the effects of the meeting (even of the fact that it takes place) on others. The VIPs who set the meeting apart may be political leaders, CEOs of big corporations, famous world-class scientists or economists, authors of best-selling books, or financial giants. They do not necessarily have to be household names, only extremely influential. The common defining word for this class of individual is "leader," sometimes "world leader," and one of their likely possessions is "charisma." A meeting attended by a big shot is his or hers alone to lord over. An assembly that includes several big shots is a gathering of significance. These VIP types are very busy people, and have endless demands on their time, so when they do commit to a meeting it means at least two things. Firstly, they believe the reason for the gathering is highly justified and secondly, they expect, and are expected, to contribute a great deal to the meeting.

The personalities of these VIPs vary from surprising modesty to obnoxious egotism. Each is aware of possessing exceptional stature, and of occupying a lofty position in life. Even if they are expert at not showing it, all sincerely believe themselves to be outstanding both in competence and in earned merit of respect. They tend to have their own meeting culture, and their own code of behavior during meetings, which stems from their appreciation of their extraordinary status.

This book has not been written for big wheels; if you are a big wheel, stop reading now. However, it is useful to contrast the rules of conduct in a VIP meeting with those in the average meeting; doing this will teach some important rules of conduct for the average meeting-goer-toer. Ordinary meetings will have attendees of varying levels of importance, and therefore different attendees will find there are different levels of results and usefulness expected of them. Typical confab members may include shy and quiet introverts, conceited asses, fools, smart-alecks, walking encyclopedias, phonies, geniuses, and those erroneously rating themselves in the celebrity category. If we are to be expert meeting-goer-toers we must learn to deal with them all.

The dynamics of a meeting are changed when a VIP attends; we other attendees are on our best behavior, we mind our manners. We are more likely to conduct ourselves in the ways we know we should behave in all meetings we attend. We are considerate of the other attendees; we always show respect for their ideas even when we disagree. But every busy meeting-goer-toer knows that the more important a get-together is to us attendees, the greater will be our desire to influence the meeting's discussion and results and press others to meet our particular desires. The presence of one or more persons of unusual stature limits the scope of aggressive behaviors in which we might otherwise engage. We are quiet and patient when a VIP speaks. If we are forced to differ we will state our points diplomatically and courteously. We will avoid using intemperate language.

The catch is that this refined behavior is not always a good thing; you should not censor yourself to the point where you are reluctant to express your true feelings for fear of contradicting the VIP. Nor should you be aggressive to the point of being "sometimes wrong but never in doubt," as this kind of behavior can be damaging if not checked. Top meeting-goer-toers are aware of the importance of regulating their behavior in a meeting, and their code of manners during meetings, stemming from confidence in their own competence, will be to offer their ideas, opinions, facts, and rationales. If they see they must, they will oppose the views of VIPs present but they will be careful how they do it. They will always prepare well, knowing that they may need to challenge a VIP should one be attending the meeting.

A Sense of Humor

Having and using common sense contributes to success in any walk of life; possessing a sense of humor is invaluable. Humor is a crucial ingredient of an attractive personality, and its offspring, wit, can be a powerful tool in meetings. Knowing how and when to use wit and humor in a meeting is an important skill, and merits attention.

Popular people are able to see the funny side of things. If you don't get the joke when humor is used in a social situation, or if you are stuck with a permanently serious demeanor, you may be admired for your knowledge, natural talent, or developed skill, but you should not expect others to delight in simply being with you.

Some "funny" people don't have the gift of being spontaneously humorous; these folks collect jokes, tell them well, and have one on tap for every occasion, so they will be welcome entertainers at times. In meetings, however, there is much more to it.

The most important and fascinating subject matter in any meeting are the attendees; because, as a humorist/philosopher once observed, "people are funnier than anybody." Demonstrate you are naturally sensitive and alert to the comical aspects of human behavior and you will be recognized as one who "gets" people. Your ability to observe the nuances of the topics under discussion and succinctly and humorously comment on them will make you look not only funny, but smart also. In contrast, people who don't get the point and who fail to comprehend what is laughable about a situation, appear "dull-witted." These people don't have humorous comments to share and are unable to respond to others' witty observations because the humor is "over their head."

To demonstrate, years ago I was at a meeting called by Scott Collins, the president of a small college. Collins was trying to interest the group, all long-time friends of his and of each other, in helping him raise a million dollars for the college's planned new library. At one point, he mentioned that the college would name the library after the donor and if two people were to share the funding then the college would place both names on the library.

Now, one of the folks at the meeting was a very rich gentleman named Raymond Scott. The two, Scott and Collins, knew each other especially well, Raymond Scott having been on the board of trustees of the college for years. To add a light touch to the meeting, President Scott Collins turned to Raymond Scott saying, "As an example, here is a proposal I'd like to make to you, my good friend Ray. I suggest you and I together put up the million dollars. We will share it in the ratio of our two personal net worths. Your wealth must be about one hundred times mine. So I'll put up ten thousand dollars and you, Ray, will donate the remaining nine hundred and ninety thousand dollars. The college will feature both our names on the library. Naturally, in recognition of your larger portion of the funds, it's only fair that your name should come first. The building will be named the 'Scott Collins Library.'"

We all laughed—except for Raymond Scott. He didn't get it. The group added some points to their esteem of President Collins and lowered their rating of Mr. Scott a bit.

Humor can be very useful when meetings become tense and angry. Someone with both the ability to see the humorous side of things and enough common sense not to attempt being funny at the wrong moment can be invaluable at such times. In fact, chances are that the more quarrelsome people get as they differ on serious issues the more abundant are humor opportunities. As people get angry, worried, and disgusted with each other they are inclined to exaggerate their statements. An overstatement by one is topped by another's and extreme statements tend to give birth to opportunities for witty commentary. A sudden interjection and recognition of the comical side then can often quell the discussion, reducing the excitement down to containable levels.

The Pill Personality

Anyone who has attended meetings by the thousands, as has the author, has invariably attended a few, either good or bad, that will never be forgotten. One meeting I attended took place years ago in the West Wing of the White House, and it comes to my mind as I write about meeting personalities.

The Chair of this meeting was a member of the President's

cabinet. The President had given him the assignment of putting together advice for action on a troubling issue and the Secretary had called a day-long meeting in the Roosevelt Room.

The Secretary did a lot of talking in the gathering. What he chose to emphasize disclosed more about him—intentionally about his life's history and unintentionally about his personality— than about the subject of the meeting. He displayed a number of characteristics that are unlikely to lead to success in meeting-going-toing. One was to take anything anyone said and use that as a basis for a little story about himself. He would ignore the irrelevance of his tale to what was being discussed and start with "That reminds me of when I. . ." Every one of these tales showed him in a highly favorable light. Did I say favorable? Words like brilliant, remarkable, and amazing would be more accurate in describing the caustic wit, or dry humor of his comments at various high-level meetings in the past.

By noon the Secretary had revealed to us that he thought himself to be a serious candidate for President at the next opportunity. He seemed very interested in being liked and he had figured out that the way to be popular was to issue compliments, at the slightest excuse, to everyone he dealt with. At this meeting, whenever one of us offered a comment the Secretary inevitably responded with a few words of congratulations on what a great contribution our expressed thought was. At one point I posed a question about whether a particular item should be added to a list placed before us. He found something in the wording of my question that he chose to label a broad, imaginative concept. He gave it a name, the "Ramo Concept," which was ludicrous. Everyone knew it and we looked around the room at each other, puzzled.

Part of the meeting time was taken up by his explaining why the President had chosen him for this assignment. Naturally, in doing so he convinced us that, important as the issue was, it was not comparable to a President's having to decide to go to war. To be qualified to Chair this meeting did not require, as he seemed to imply, someone describable as a combination of the best of Lincoln and Einstein. None of us at the meeting, although we all could be called established experts in various areas pertinent to the meeting's subject, were VIP's known to be such to the general public. So the Secretary had no competition in this meeting. As I listened to him demonstrate his sincere admiration of himself with his every pontification I wondered what would happen if two such narcissistic "world leaders" chanced to be in the same meeting.

The Lowbrow Attendee

Most meetings don't include many such big wheels. On the contrary most meetings will be handicapped by the presence of low, not high personages. Suppose a participant in a meeting becomes an intolerable nuisance, interrupting others, loudly belaboring points he makes, and insisting on monopolizing the discussion. He carries on too long when he comments, generally combining bad manners with serious time wasting. Though he may not be the lowlife his lousy personality and manners suggest he is incompetent with no realization of that shortcoming.

What might the Chair do to curb him and prevent him from impeding the progression of the meeting? Most often the Chair has no choice but to try to shut him up one way or another. In this instance, the other attendees won't mind. They'll up their rating of the Chair's conduct. What is considered good behavior and what is considered the opposite of it varies widely with the situation. Manners have to be defined by the context, not by a generality.

The MDRSSA

What kind of personality—not what individual—is the worst I have ever encountered in a meeting? No question at all: the most painful, frustrating meeting-goer-toer is the *Multi-Dimensional Really Smart Smart-Ass* (MDRSSA). This person is unquestionably very sharp on almost anything that comes up in a meeting and, at the same time, has strong views about every issue. Most annoyingly, the MDRSSA is close to being always right. A discussion of the MDRSSA is essential, if only to warn those readers who are possessed of super-minds and who might become, but must positively resolve not to allow themselves to become, MDRSSAs.

First let us add some details to clarify what kind of person we are discussing. An ordinary smart-ass or a smart-aleck is one who pretends to smartness. The smart-aleck may not be dumb, but huge pretension masks his smartness, whatever its degree. A smart-ass in a meeting can be insufferable, but only a truly extreme smart-ass who is smart beyond belief and knows it can be the ruiner of a meeting and of it's participants' composure. Of course an MDRSSA will know it. How can he or she not know it? And is it at all realistic to assume that MDRSSAs will not manifest mega-conceit? An MDRSSA is extremely pretentious and smart and overly anxious to display it. It is impossible to imagine a more negative personality.

When in a meeting with a MDRSSA you may conclude there are no advantages to this individual's presence, but some benefits do exist. MDRSSA's are quick to alert their fellow meeting-goers to any fact of even the slightest relevance to the meeting; errors in data or reasoning are exposed by an MDRSSA promptly. All useful alternatives for action on each issue are laid out for consideration in no time. Clear conclusions are reached speedily and meetings rarely go into overtime, in fact they will often adjourn early.

The MDRSSA described above would attain a hundred on the negative personality score, luckily I have not actually suffered through a meeting with one who scores so high, but I have had the misfortune of running across several in the nineties and that was bad enough. In the company of an MDRSSA with a rating of ninety, the chance of your making your day by showing that MDRSSA to be wrong on something—or of your coming up with a better suggestion to counter the MDRSSA's proposal on any meeting question—is small.

If you, the reader, see yourself as having an intellectual capacity equal that of an MDRSSA, if you possess both the gall and braininess required for membership in that peculiarly small club, then try, do please try, to avoid developing the bad parts.

Poor Losers

The last unpleasant personality type you may find in a meeting is the poor loser. Poor losers are always poor meeting-goer-toers, and any meeting participant who frequently displays this unattractive personality element will lose respect every time he demonstrates it. When you win a debate from him, he will feel much more unhappiness and ill will towards you than mere disappointment would justify. The Poor Loser will be unable to suppress or hide his sudden dislike of you and others will note such offensive behavior and think less of the loser—his manners will be judged as truly bad. Poor Losers are likely to exhibit hurt feelings whenever another meeting participant says something even slightly and justifiably critical of him or his commentary. Poor Losers are also prone to be egotistical, which often means their ideas and reasoning are limited as they refuse to accept others' ideas. And they simply can't stand to be seen as wrong about anything.

One rule here is clear. Never be a Poor Loser.

We have dwelt on these bad personality traits because it's likely that each of us contains a little of one of them in our nature. These characteristics are inherent in us, but we normally have them under good control. When we experience embarrassment, disappointment, inadequacy, or failure in our performance during a meeting our confidence and comfort may be temporarily lowered to the point that it causes us to display the bad sides of our personalities. We meeting-goer-toers must develop the discipline to restrict the disclosing of the less admirable dimensions of our makeups. It is a sign of wisdom and maturity if we learn to control them. It will pay off in ensuring a steady high level of meeting-going-toing success.

The Attire Dimension

Good manners in a meeting involve more than how you act. Your appearance in a meeting affects how you are perceived, and your influence on the meeting's results can be impaired if you make serious mistakes in your attire. So let us next discuss how you dress for a meeting. At the least you should avoid the obvious botches. Let us list a few:

◇ Don't deviate widely in your attire from the norms set by the majority of your fellow meeting attendees.

◇ Wild, dirty hair is out, even if many meeting attendees seem, by their own chosen hairdos, not to care. Play it safe by washing and combing.

◇ Never overdress. Keep it down.

◇ If the boss shows up at a meeting wearing a U.S. State Department wide-striped shirt with a stiff starched separate white collar, don't show up at the next meeting with the same ensemble.

◇ If you have super-bulging arm muscles don't don short-sleeved shirts.

◇ Never wear a miniskirt to a meeting, even if you are slim and young (especially if you are sexy). Ditto for tight leather pants.

◇ Don't set records in the heel-height category.

◇ If you sweat profusely and need to change shirts hourly to keep from looking abhorrent, cover yourself with a very lightweight jacket. (You'll perspire more, but fewer will notice.)

◇ The pervasive police dramas on TV feature women detectives with terrific figures all wearing very tight sweaters. Even if you are similarly endowed, recognize that your meetings are not TV programs.

◇ Neatness suggests maturity and seriousness. Others will listen to what you say if you look neat.

◇ Sloppiness suggests you don't care about yourself and are lazy. If you appear to have a low evaluation of yourself others will not rate you higher.

◇ Care in your dressing elevates the occasion. If you are a presenter at a meeting your audience will be less attentive if you take less interest in how you look.

◇ A meeting is not a good platform for launching creative breakthroughs in clothes. (Marlene Dietrich and Katherine Hepburn enhanced their fame by pioneering the wearing of trousers by women. But that was show business, the key word being "show.")

◇ Remember that how you dress tells everyone something about you, especially about your personality.

Many things in your genes and your life will determine your personality. To be a top performer in meetings it is essential that you rate the developing of an attractive personality of critical importance. If you really want to, you can.

The Gender Factor

The earlier chapter on meeting chairing mentioned the preju-dices of some people against female Chairs; the bias factor in meeting-going-toing is complex and important enough an area of human relations to deserve a chapter of its own. Prejudice is a fac-tor in every endeavor in which people are engaged—it is an inher-ent characteristic of the human race. A white professor, for example, might change colleges if a black professor is made Dean over him. A big fellow may quit rather than work under a physi-cally small man promoted to be his boss. A man close to retire-ment age may choose to retire early rather than report to a new supervisor who is only thirty. There are numerous such types of bias. In this chapter, however, we shall confine the discussion to gender biases as they affect meeting-going-toing.

The Ideal?

In meetings gender issues and all real and imagined differences between males and females should play no part in the attendees' t of their duties. Meetings are called for specific reasons and e participants should be chosen because they fill the specific needs of each conference. The selecting of meeting attendees and their roles should be unrelated to whether they happen to be male or female. If a meeting should involve, say, an engineer, an auditor, a marketing expert, or a personnel recruiter, those partakers should be picked for their expertise regardless of their genders. Of course, situations will exist where a gender issue is actually a meeting agenda item. A meeting might be called, for instance, to hear someone report a harassment problem. We are not concerned here with such matters. What we shall discuss in this chapter are improper biases that affect meetings when they should not do so.

In this new century the concept of no gender prejudice is being applied successfully in a substantial fraction of all meetings. This favorable trend applies to the choosing of the Chair and the other attendees, the setting of the agenda, and the overall conducting of the meeting. Too often, however, this ideal is far from being actually attained and a professional meeting-goer-toer must understand that.

As we strive to develop a meeting culture that houses no gender prejudices, it would be a mistake not to acknowledge that real differences between male and female humans actually do exist. Males behave differently towards females than toward fellow males and visa versa; if there are no women at the meeting you are unlikely to see the men standing and fiddling with the chairs to assist in the seating of their male neighbors. They won't watch their language as they speak. They will not hold back telling a joke that fits the situation well but is badly off-color. They will express their disagreements with fellow meeting participants freely and sometimes even violently. These behaviors are much more likely to be censored if some of the attendees are women.

Centuries of indoctrination have trained men to be chivalrous and more considerate with females than with other males. It is as unlikely that this kind of "good" bias will ever fully change as it is that the "bad" bias will completely end, even as women equal or surpass their male coworkers. After all, there are biological differences between the sexes—women who become pregnant are far more likely to find their work affected by this than are their male counterparts who find their wives are expecting. Most women meeting-goer-toers, upon becoming pregnant, will continue to attend meetings. As the pregnancy becomes noticeable they will receive seating preferences from men plus priorities in entering elevators. They will be spoken to gently by fellow meeting-goer-toers. This pattern of behavior toward pregnancy probably will continue forever in time.

Sexual Distractions

NEVER WEAR A MINISKIRT TO A MEETING

Though any professional should know better, flirting and even sexual relationships can be initiated in a meeting. Such things occur and we should not attribute them exclusively to young people who lack the experience and discretion to understand that the work arena is an unsuitable place to look for a romantic partner. Older people are also prone to sizing up individuals of the opposite sex with whom they are in contact as potential partners. Allowing sex into the workplace is a potential problem for both sexes in mixed company, but there are great differences in how male and female meeting-goer-toers are affected by it.

Take, for example, the subject of meeting attire, touched on for other reasons in an earlier chapter. Prime time television offers many drama and comedy series which inevitably include a generous offering of sexy women. You will also notice that their attire clearly has been selected to emphasize their physical rather than professional appeal. The male characters, whether chosen for specific TV roles because of their physical attributes or not, are clothed less imaginatively. Clothes may make the man, but it is highly improbable that a male meeting-attendee could ever devise an outfit that would be deemed inappropriate due to its "sexiness." Whether they want to or not, women attendees are much more likely to provide information about the shape of their flesh and bones by the way they dress. Indeed women's body shapes are difficult to hide by clothes unless the meeting is held in Saudi Arabia. If you are a woman headed for a meeting, you must understand that your male coworkers are likely to see you—if only for a subconscious second—as a sexual object, no matter how hard you try to disguise this.

The truth is a very attractive woman can upset a meeting. The men present may concentrate their minds more on her than on the meeting's agenda items and the other women present will loathe the sexy gal and will look forward to the pleasure of discussing her with the other ladies after the meeting. A female participant with high sexual attraction who is not dressed to downplay it will, at a minimum, exact a disruption tax on the meeting's business.

Women meeting-goer-toers pay more attention to the attire of other attendees, both male and female, than do men. If men notice what women wear in a meeting it's because of the sex appeal of the outfit; a voluptuous body beneath an outfit is more interesting to men than the outfit's style, coordination with accessories, or lack of either. If a man admires a skirt it's more likely due to it's brevity than the richness of the fabric. A male attendee with executive responsibilities may notice in a meeting how the other attendees are dressed. He will look for appropriateness. If it is the custom that male attendees come to the meeting with jackets and ties then he will spot the exceptions. Women executives will do the same, but will go further.

A woman views a man's attire as offering useful clues to his personality, character, and background. Is he neat or sloppy? Is he bold, artistic, dull, careless, peacockish, interesting, precise, imaginative—in short, what's he like as a person? Is he a possible future associate, husband, lover, boss, or assistant? Women judge all this in part by the way a man dresses.

Women will have stronger opinions and will be more likely to voice them with the other women attendees about violations of their dress code. Admittedly, a man may notice whether a woman attendee at a meeting is overly casual or overdressed. But his disdain for a female in the wrong clothes will be limited compared with his female counterpart. She will immediately rate down not merely the taste in clothes but also the intelligence and sophistication of any woman in the meeting whose outfit feels dated or inappropriate.

A man looking at another man's jacket, slacks, shirt, and tie, and perhaps noting they clash, will give it at most a passing glance and assessment. A woman observing that same man's unsynchronized getup will give him a general bad mark that will stay in her memory about him forever. A middle-aged, overweight woman with fat legs and an overly noticeable bottom who shows up in too short a skirt will cause a male attendee to look away. A woman viewer will judge that erring lady dresser not only as unlucky in her body, but more importantly, as stupid, and will not take seriously her contributions to the meeting.

Meeting Weeping

At some point in a meeting you will be involved in a discussion about whether a woman could ever be elected as President. Someone, male or female, will inevitably claim that women do not possess the emotional strength needed and that when the burdens of responsibility peak severely, she will break down and cry. This common belief has not been shattered by the fact that Britain, Israel, India, and several other nations have or have had women top executives, each with records of strong leadership under the most trying of circumstances.

The bias that says women cannot stand up under extreme stress is applied to more positions of authority than just the Presidency. It is a serious factor in the choosing of business leaders, university heads, law firm presidents, or hospital directors, and even applies in the selecting of Chairs for meetings. Meetings that involve pressure-laden issues and awful attendee personalities can quickly degenerate into angry, tense events—frazzled nerves, ill tempers, and ill will may set the meeting tone. Opponents will argue their positions with anger, passion and a total lack of tact or respect for feelings. If hectic circumstances are expected for a meeting, all participants naturally will feel that a very strong, emotionally firm Chair is mandatory. To curb the strain on all participants, the Chair must above all be tough and cool. So the Chair cannot be a woman. She may cry.

Ruling out women to handle highly charged situations is a prejudice, and though I've never seen a study that proves this I'm confident there are no statistics proving that either men or women are better at handling pressure. I am guessing that a generalization is out of order. Here is why. People react to extreme psychological pressure in a wide variety of ways; and the breadth of different reactions taken at random will transcend the typical differences between "average" males and "average" females. Whether a leader cries or not is a reaction involving many different details about the situation and that specific person. To believe something strongly when it is clearly hard to define and prove, and has not been proven, is to be prejudiced.

Nevertheless, it is true that many meeting-goer-toers would prefer a male to a female Chair for a difficult meeting because of the level of expected discord and anxiety. Similarly, many more people believe that women, far more than men, will react by weeping when subjected to severe emotional stress. Suppose, for the sake of argument, we grant that. What does it necessarily tell us about the leadership qualities of a man (who will likely not cry) as compared with a woman (who might)? To demonstrate how difficult it may be to assess the power of tears to influence control in a meeting, I cannot resist citing my personal experience with meetings where someone has been brought to tears. The majority of the tens of thousands of meetings I have attended were happy, quiet, and unemotional. Some were filled with great stress of every kind from difficult decision making to the interrelating of competitive and unfriendly attendees. Only once in my seventy years of meetings did anyone ever break down and cry.

It was a man, a rocket scientist in fact, who reached that level of personal emotional distress. For weeks he had been under tremendous pressure to solve the mystery of why, under some circumstances, the rocket engine for whose development he was responsible would fail. It would operate perfectly most of the time, then mysteriously, with no quantifiable detail of its operation altered, it would malfunction. That flaw was holding up a high priority military project's completion. He lost sleep day after day as, determined to keep his high-priority project on schedule, he tracked down every clue about that engine's design malfunction.

Finally he solved the problem. He was able to present all the evidence and explain the fault and its proven cure to his peers. Completely exhausted, he nevertheless stood up for over an hour, made a totally convincing presentation, and answered all questions completely. The top project director then asked for applause and congratulated him on his outstanding engineering achievement and his personal devotion and commitment. The rocket scientist wanted to simply stand and say "thank you." Instead, after a failed attempt to speak, he let loose with a noisy stream of sobs and tears. That he cried surprised us, but it didn't matter to us. We all thought he was great.

I don't know what that incident proves. And that is the point. Bias against women being made leaders in potentially emotionally charged circumstances remain.[4]

---

[4] In the interest of full disclosure, I must add that in one additional meeting in my life an attendee was heard to weep. It was a meeting of the Salt Lake City Ladies Literary Club in 1921. After the regular review of books, a short musical performance was the meeting pattern. At age 8, I was the soloist for that meeting. I played a movement of a Bach sonata for violin alone, a piece chock full of notes to be played very fast. I played every note up to speed. Each note was badly off key. This time the weeper was a lady—my music teacher.

The Token Woman

An excellent illustration of the nature and status of bias against women in meetings is the "token woman" phenomenon, which began to be noticeable about a half century ago. Diminished with the passing decades, the "token women" can still be found with saddening regularity today. In the mid-twentieth century it was exceedingly rare to find a woman on any board of directors of a large corporation, or as a member of the board of trustees of a prestigious private university, or on the top staffs of hospitals or of prominent law and accounting firms. Women rarely served on principal government advisory committees, or as a member of the U.S. Senate, or the House of Representatives, or the Supreme Court, or even of a lower level governing assembly like a city council.

Suppose you were on the Board of Directors of a large publicly held business corporation a half-century ago. Let's say you were on the nominating committee as well and you were determined to add a woman member to that board, thus breaking past precedents. (That was my personal experience more than once). At that time you would be aware that all present members of that board were principal executives of other large companies or retired major executives. A director here and there might have been head of a large accounting, law, or banking firm. Typically, a lawyer on the board at that time expected to do work for the company, ditto the accountants and bankers. A few board members during that period might not have had background in direct managing of businesses but then they would have been distinguished in their fields. They would have been the president of a higher-education institution, or a big-name economist, or a Nobel award-level scientist. A few decades ago it was rare to find a woman in any of these special categories.

If you were seeking female board candidates at that time you would look first for a lady who was a principal executive of some other large industrial corporation, just the way you were accustomed to do in filling a board opening with a man. But there were too few women CEOs of the top thousand U.S. corporations. As few as five might have had a woman as a principal executive in those days and two of those would have been the presidents of cosmetics firms they founded. With all 995 other corporations wanting a token woman board member, any woman even close to filling the pertinent CEO experience requirement would already have had dozens of board invitations. With maybe five women candidates to consider, you would find that three had already accepted board memberships with competitors and were thus ineligible. The other two probably would have no practical chance to schedule proper meeting attendance on your board because they would already have become a member of too many other boards.

At that time most people realized that it would be at least twenty years before there would be enough eligible candidates to allow most large publicly held corporations to actually meet the "token woman" goal. It would take that long for the younger women who were just starting out in the increasingly egalitarian business world to mature and advance to the higher management posts. Only then would they have become eligible for large corporation board membership without a lowering of the standards as to the required years of management accomplishment.

Now that amount of time has passed and the number of publicly held business corporations that have found a female to bring onto their board is substantial. The same can be said for the big charitable foundations and for leadership groups in academics, government, and the professions. In the new century most entities have their one woman and a few of them have been able even to capture more than one. No large corporation today, however, has women as half or more of its members. We can say the same of trustees of universities and other leading nonprofit organizations. To find organizations with a majority of women on the boards we would have to include knitting and quilt-making clubs.

The Odd Member

Consider the difficulties faced by the first woman to sit on the board of directors of a major business corporation. Imagine her sitting with a dozen men and pretending nonchalance when she was aware of these facts:

◇ She had been elected to the board not because she was considered eminently capable, though she may have been thought to be by those who chose her and by her own self-rating. Rather she was there because it seemed important the corporation have a female director.

◇ She was not a member of the "club," the fraternity of principal executives of corporations who talk in their special code, play golf with each other, belong to the same clans, sit on each others boards, set each others compensation, and tell the same kind of jokes for men only.

◇ Never having been on such a board she was not completely familiar with the corporate board culture. She was not aware what motions a board member expects to automatically vote "yea" on and never question, what are the customary prerogatives of CEOs and board members, what kind of questions about operations and plans are expected from board members, when a lengthy commentary is in or out of order, and numerous other such director's meeting patterns. She was perplexed to find that she was stared at many times as topics came up and comments were made by the male directors. Was it because they simply wanted to confirm that she probably did not know what they were talking about, or were they expecting a reaction from her?

Over the decades, I have attended a rather large number of meetings of boards and committees whose members initially were all male. Most of those meetings have advanced to have one (fortunate or unfortunate) lady member. I have come to know many female corporate executives that made it to the top in business, and all were outstanding. I have known women senators and women presidents of leading universities. I have danced at a party with a female member of the U.S. Supreme Court. Bias against women is far less now than a half-century ago when real change first began. Some remaining biases will last for a long time before they die out. Certain inherent differences between the two sexes will exist forever and will continue to influence meetings.

Distractions and Disruptions

A seasoned meeting-goer-toer understands that meetings may be disturbed by the unplanned, unnecessary, and annoying activities of other attendees. It's like watching an interesting and informative TV program that is interrupted every ten minutes by a grating and irrelevant commercial—we know we must tolerate the commercials if we want to enjoy TV. However, unlike the passive TV viewer, meeting attendees can fight back against interruption and can minimize meeting distractions if they understand the how and why of them. We hope in this chapter to help the reader do that by citing an array of disruptions that occur frequently in meetings.

The Note-Taker

Many meeting-goer-toers cannot attend a meeting without bringing a pad or tablet. They sit and take notes—presumably to set down what others are saying or thoughts or questions they think

of during the meeting. Some just doodle; everyone should have a hobby and a bit of fantasizing by pen is helpful to some at times. However, compulsive doodling during a meeting suggests a lack of interest in the meeting's agenda on the part of the doodler. If you are a compulsive doodler—if you can't sit and listen and contribute during a meeting—if you use the meeting only to develop your visual artistic talents—then you probably should not be an attendee. However, should you come and doodle, your contribution to the meeting may be trivial, but at least it will not disrupt it.

A really annoying distraction in a meeting is the special class of note-taker who feverishly writes down every syllable uttered in the meeting just as a court reporter is assigned to do. With his head constantly down and eyes glued to his pad rather than directed at the attendees who are speaking, his pen traverses the paper madly. This obsessed note-taker's facial expression depicts his determination to miss nothing no matter how rapid the speaker's delivery is. All attendees will notice such super-active recording. Indeed many may choose to interest themselves more in the race between the speaker's outflow of words and the note-taker's finger movements than in the meeting's discussion. The meeting's focus will then have moved away from what should have been the center of attention.

It can be worse. I cite a personal experience. Once in a certain meeting I was required to make some comments dealing with classified military subject matter. Everyone present was cleared for the appropriate high secrecy level. I had noticed earlier that one attendee was a note-taker with an unusually avid devotion to tablet and pen. To my relief, he happened to be in an inactive, quiet phase as I began to speak. Then suddenly, he grabbed his pen and began to write with enormous vigor and speed and a new look of seriously committed concentration. Was it something I just said? Something wrong? Something I should not have disclosed to this group because it was of higher secrecy classification than the meeting's clearance level? Did the little glance he shot at me mean, "Ah-ha! You will be sorry you said that!"

But why should I be so fearful? Maybe he thought my speech was great! Maybe it deserved to be recorded! Maybe he is going to quote me in some proper place, to my credit!

What about the other attendees? I see now that they have picked up on the note-taker's sudden busyness. All eyes are on him. What are they thinking? Oops! Now they are looking at me! Then back to him! They are curious as to my reaction to the note-taker! The more I watch him the poorer my choice of words was and the lower the clarity and emphasis of my presentation.

Distraction! Distraction! Distraction!

Coffee

Consider another very different source of meeting disturbance. Smoking has virtually been eliminated as a problem for meeting-goer-toers who don't smoke. Sure, we still have to tolerate brief absences by those few remaining smokers as they slip out to get their fix. Ashamed of still smoking, they try to do so unnoticed, hoping we'll assume they've gone to the phone or the lavatory. As a distraction, smoking is now trivial. But coffee drinking—that's a big item.

The coffee habit is not like smoking. No one suffers from secondhand caffeine. Too much coffee may be bad for those hooked on it, but a meeting attendee's drinking even ten cups during a long meeting will not keep other conferees from sleeping that night. The harm, if any, is only to the imbiber. We discuss coffee drinking here because it goes on so pervasively, is a permanent fixture in meetings, and can cause meeting distractions.

Watch any Humphrey Bogart motion picture and notice how he never answers immediately no matter what anyone says to him. Instead he slowly gets out a pack of cigarettes, calmly extracts one, and fits it carefully between his lips just so. He ceremoniously produces a match, ignites it with cool deftness, and lights the cigarette artistically. Smoothly he inhales a few puffs and takes his time before exhaling dramatically. All the while we are convinced that he is contemplating in depth his eventual answer to the other actor's comment or question, a rejoinder we now anticipate, with growing excitement, hearing momentarily. This episode is repeated a dozen times. This routine forms a good part of the movie.

Notice at your next meeting how some attendees perform a similar act with a cup of coffee. They start a comment, or indicate one is coming from them, and simultaneously arise from their chairs. They look around to spot the right container, regular or decaf. They commandeer a mug or cup. They pour the coffee with concentration. They leisurely but deliberately add cream or sugar and carefully stir their beverage just so. They raise the cup to their lips, cautiously, because the coffee may be hot. The first sip is tiny and tentative, followed after a brief pause, the cup still held close to the mouth, by a still small, second tasting. The now coffee-equipped individual next moves to rejoin the meeting. We watch as the mug is set down at the right place and the drinker gets himself seated, filled with expectation as to what will come next.

Everyone present accepts this procedure without considering the time it takes—but imagine a meeting attendee behaving in such a way *without* a cup of coffee as a prop. If you were to fail to make a comment for such a period of time while others waited expectantly for it—people would assume you were perplexed. They would figure that you don't know the answer to the question put to you, or you don't understand the comment that led to your being expected to reply, or you can't figure out what you should say. Respect for you would be diminished—but not if you perform your little coffee playlet using up the same block of time. In fact, the more skillfully you perform your coffee act, the greater the respect you generate.

But there's more: the constant refill activity of the coffee pots, the getting up and down of the attendees for the replenishing, the polite inquiries as to whether a cup should be brought to a seated neighbor as long as one is already going for coffee, and then the reseating. All this is a distraction that affects the entire meeting—not just the coffee drinkers—by diverting their attention towards the activity at the coffee table and away from the matters at hand.

Of course, why stop with coffee? The ice clinking in water pitchers, water bottles, glasses, cans of diet drink, oatmeal cookies, and doughnuts cause meeting disturbances. But coffee is the star, the only player in the cast with the certainty of permanence.

Cell Phones

Cell phones are marvelous conveniences when used by oneself; when employed by others seated near us they become monstrous ruiners of our environment. *We*, of course, only answer our cell phones because it might be an emergency. *We* originate calls only when we find it necessary. It is difficult for us to understand why others can be so gross and inconsiderate as to foist their sensitive personal conversations on everyone in their immediate vicinity.

What's wrong with the following statement?

In meetings cell phones are never problems. In meetings they never produce distractions. That is because all attendees turn off their phones and never allow them to ring during any meeting. If a vibrator replaces a ringer, no attendee ever answers and talks.

Really? Not here on Earth! On another planet perhaps.

A few weeks before I wrote this, I happened to chair a meeting with a group of about twenty, one of whom, Hardy, was in the middle of an important presentation including a series of complex screen projections in a somewhat darkened room. Suddenly,

Stanley, one of my fellow listeners, received, and *answered,* a call on his cell phone. Even more gallingly he greeted his caller in his normal speaking voice rather than the more appropriate whisper. We all thought Stanley would get up and leave the room with his cell phone, indeed Hardy stopped her presentation, expecting the interference would be temporary.

But, to our amazement Stanley, proceeded to carry on a loud conversation. After waiting a few moments Hardy decided that we would not pay attention to Stanley, so she continued with her presentation. They immediately constituted a disharmonious duet for the listeners' ears. As the Chair, I chose to address Hardy, not Stanley. In a loud voice I said "Would you please stop your presentation, Hardy, because, if you go right on speaking, we won't be able to hear clearly Stanley's phone conversation!"

Hardy heard this, stopped talking, and we all looked at Stanley who we knew could not help but hear my request to Hardy. Stanley looked puzzled for an instant then said into his phone "Please hold a minute," and left the room with his cell phone. When some fifteen minutes later Stanley returned to his seat the rest of us pretended not to notice.

Call Backs

We don't have to depend upon the modern cell phone to disrupt meetings—the old-fashioned wired telephone system still provides ample opportunities. Many meeting attendees who don't bring live cell phones into a meeting nevertheless cannot run their lives without maintaining contact with their staffs, homes, business associates, and others. When they arrive at a meeting they immediately place calls, leaving messages telling where they are and requesting a callback. Unsurprisingly the meeting-going-toers who do this get callbacks during the meeting. They have adopted this procedure for many diverse reasons. (One of which, we suspect, is to look important to the other attendees.)

Mark is an exceptionally devout practitioner of this "call back" practice. During any meeting Mark attends, the following one-act dramatic scenario will be played out. The door into the meeting room opens slightly, just enough for all of us at the meeting to

ONE OF MARK'S CALL-BACKS HAS ARRIVED

spot a secretary peering in and holding a note. Chances are she cannot readily identify Mark, the meeting participant she is seeking. She thus has to move on in. She is noticed by all to be trying to do so unnoticed. She goes to the nearest attendee who she sees is looking at her and asks in a whisper "Which is Mr. Mark?" and she then goes to Mark and hands him the note with a few words (which we can't hear, darn it!).

Whoever is speaking in the meeting at the moment has lost his audience. We are all wondering what Mark will do? We watch intently to learn the answer. What does his face show? Is Mark startled, frightened, angry, happy, or puzzled by the message? Is he calm, or is his hand trembling? Will he whisper that he'll call back? Will he leave the meeting and go take the call? Will he whisper to the secretary an answer of sorts to be passed on to the caller? Will he write a message and hand it to the secretary? What if he just takes the note without even looking at it and sets the little paper on the table, it's words face down, and ignores it? What could that mean? What's it all about? We'd like to know! Shucks! We apparently are not going to know! So, reluctantly, back to the meeting. Now, where were we before this distraction started?

Attendees with Libraries

Meeting attendees often arrive at a meeting with a document or two that they place on the conference table. Usually it is a neat little pile, disturbed in the meeting only occasionally and rather quietly and carefully. The attendee may look up something in the documents during the meeting, or jot a quick note in the margins of his paperwork.

Picture now the extremist, like my fellow meeting-goer-toer Raymond. He always arrives at a meeting with a very large briefcase from which he extracts a collection of folders, a book, some journals, and a motley pile of memos which he then deposits on the conference table. No one can escape noticing, and all inevitably stop what they are doing and take in the unpleasant sight. Judging from past performances, Raymond will soon become busy manipulating his library. Opening, closing, shuffling, restacking— Raymond will be steadily occupied with managing his paperwork during the meeting. In fact Raymond will be so busy with this task that he won't appear to be listening or looking up as others speak. As the meeting progresses Raymond will become more and more absorbed with making notes in his paperwork, and looking up details that he inevitably finds ten minutes too late to be useful. The physical appearance of Raymond's data menagerie continues to deteriorate as it takes up more and more table space.

Laptops

Raymond established himself years ago, early in his meeting-going-toing life, as one who cannot attend a meeting without bringing along his disruptive reference library. But he is outdone now by the younger Miss Miller. Miller brings her laptop to every meeting she attends. Her computer extends the meeting distraction potential. True, with her we are not bothered by a repulsive pile of paper products on the table. A neat piece of equipment is now in its place. But Miller, our modern avid information-loving disrupter of meetings, is constantly tapping at her computer. It is almost impossible for other attendees not to watch as Miller furiously presses keyboard keys as rapidly as Vladimir Horowits when performing a Rachmaninoff concerto on the piano keys. All through the meeting Miller is mesmerized by her computer display. She studies it intently as she shifts her mouse about quickly and hits more keys. Her eyes never stray toward attendees who are speaking and pointing at charts. She never looks up at members who are debating or at the Chair who is commenting. Computerized attendee Miller is off in some "virtual" meeting, one taking place in another dimension.

What is she seeing on her computer display that leads to such insistent pressure for her to program and reprogram it towards further displays? What information is Miller entering or calling up with such fervor? What does this computer activity have to do with the meeting? We don't know and we won't find out. But we can't take our eyes off of it.

Recently Miller has started leaving her laptop at her office and bringing handheld equipment to the meeting. She holds the instrument in her right hand palm—at seat level where she thinks we can't see it. She can hold it and press keys all with one hand. All meeting long we observe her never looking up, concentrating her gaze down and to the right at the little display by her right knee.

Private Conversers

The sharing of information can distract in other ways as well. Whether you are speaking to the assembled group or listening to some other attendees' remarks, few things can be more annoying than when two other attendees sitting next to each other engage in private conversation. Stanley and Bates, who shared a government advisory committee with me for four years, did this bad-manner act continually during every meeting. Stanley or Bates would lean sideways to whisper into the other's ear and get a whispered response. I could never hear what was said but "whisper static" reached my ears incessantly. It was doubly irritating to know that something was being said yet not be able to make out anything from the conversation. Everyone in the meeting noticed the behavior of Stanley and Bates, and it was obvious that neither of these two sideways conversers could be concentrating on what

was going on in the meeting. The fact that Stanley and Bates seemed to think that the meeting discussion was not worth listening to bothered the other attendees. It was even more annoying when one or another of us chose to speak during the meeting and had to compete against the whispered competition. Both Stanley and Bates were judged to be people of deficient manners. The possible excuse that their whispers were so urgent they could not wait was unacceptable because, if they were that important, they should have been disclosed to the entire group. We all lowered our ratings of both Stanley and Bates.

Gigglers

Another pair of meeting-goer-toers, Harris and Williams, found another way to disrupt meetings. They would sit side by side and whisper comments to each other for no other purpose than to get a laugh. The other attendees would observe this and wonder what could be so funny. Was it something a speaker had just said? Were they making fun of us other conferees? We did not admire them for their ability to find humor in inappropriate situations, and ultimately their need to amuse each other backfired on them. We judged their giggling distasteful, and their punishment was that they were never taken seriously in meetings.

Advice: do not engage in whispered messages during meetings, especially wisecracks. While we are on the general subject, do not pass little notes to other attendees either.

Alcoholics

As in other facets of life alcoholics are more than mere annoyances in meetings. They present a problem to themselves, of course, but in a gathering of sober people intent on accomplishing serious business they can be unacceptably disruptive. Some pertinent things are easy to recommend:

⬦ If you are the Chair and are choosing the attendees, never invite a known alcoholic.

⬦ If you are asked to participate in a meeting where you know an alcoholic will be present and, judging from previous experience, will get into the act, don't accept.

⬦ If you know yourself to be an alcoholic, don't go to a meeting unless certain you will be securely sober during the relevant period, starting with before the meeting starts.

⬦ If you discover at a confab that an attendee appears drunk or adequately under the influence to impair his participation, do all you can to bypass him.

⬦ Learn to recognize when ordinary drinkers are becoming alcoholics. Alcoholics are folks who must consume many drinks daily and can't stop after the first one.

The above commentary suggests you do all you can to keep alcoholics out of the act. That may sound simple. Simplistic is what it really is because not all heavy drinkers are alcoholics. Some drinkers are not always adversely affected by their drinking habits in their meeting performances. Over the decades I have encountered plenty of meeting-goer-toers who drank heavily. Many, I must report, operated for years before it noticeably ruined their ability to contribute to or chair meetings. Some had life patterns in which they typically would be sober all day, overdrink at dinner, then continue on with nightcap after nightcap and go to bed drunk. Yet they were somehow sober and bright at the next morning's meeting.

Many substantial alcohol consumers should not be judged as alcoholics because they can stop when they so choose. Some can go on weekend binges occasionally and be sober in between. Some drinkers with big liquor appetites and high capacities for it occupy important positions, are excellent Chairs of consequential meetings, and have never been known to be late to a meeting or be tipsy or slur speech while in one. Their participation may be critical to decision-making and yet you can count on them in a meeting. However, if we go out to dinner with them after the meeting someone always has to see that they get home safely.

What can you—a teetotaler or a social drinker—do to ensure you are never placed in a difficult situation by heavy drinkers when chairing or attending a meeting,? You should recognize that the value of the sobriety-challenged, but otherwise important, participants in a meeting must be weighed against the possibility of their causing a disruption. If you cannot tolerate the risk that "tolerable" drinkers may turn "intolerable," try to delete them from meeting lists.

Late Arrivers

Late arrivers are distracting and unpopular with meeting attendees, but we all understand if fellow meeting-goer-toers sometimes arrive late. Most meetings take place in cities and all cities have severe traffic problems. Potential delays such as unpredictable jams, accidents, road repairs, ambulances and fire engines mean that your actual travel time can vary wildly. That means if you aim to be on time to a meeting you should actually aim to arrive early. The only thing you can do is be prepared to use that chunk of pre-meeting time to read, think out valuable thoughts, or update something on your laptop.

Considerate late arrivers sneak in and take their seats quietly.

The situation was far different for Kathleen or "Late Kate," as she was called by her fellow trustees of a certain university.

Late Kate was a very intelligent lady. For many years she was one of the most active members of the University's various working committees. She was simultaneously very involved with the advisory committee for the Medical School, the Buildings Committee, and numerous ad-hoc groups that would handle temporary problems and would come and go. She was a crucial participant in getting important things done and, being rather wealthy, a substantial financial contributor to the numerous causes identified with the many committees on which she served.

There was just one big problem with Late Kate; she never came to a meeting on time. The most accurate estimate of her arrival time would be at least half an hour after the typical two-hour meeting had begun. Moreover, she always had a reason to leave the meeting somewhat early, before adjournment. The Chair and the other participants had to endure not only the distraction of her tardy arrival but her insistence on individually greeting the other members. Then after finding a seat and settling into it, she would offer a detailed reason to the whole gathering of why she was late and why it could not have been avoided and would not happen again. And, of course, when she arose to leave before the meeting was over, she disrupted the meeting once more with a full recital of why she could not stay longer.

I must emphasize that, despite Late Kate's deserving nickname, during the entire long period in which she was active—middle age to elderly—her standing as a valuable trustee remained high. When she was in a meeting she was bright, well informed, showed understanding and creativity, and analyzed problems on an equal with any other member present. In addition she was a charmer. She was especially liked in the way she considered other's views. She was a lady with charisma and a meeting-goer-toer with wisdom.

But what was one to do about her disturbing of meetings as she came and went? Chairs would try. One Chair tried to figure out which agenda items Late Kate would be most interested in and then would start the meetings with those issues, completing them before Kate arrived. The Chair was willing to lose the benefits of her participation on those aspects as he attempted by this strategy to change her and make her arrive on time. That failed, of course. When she finally sat down, she would look at the agenda and see immediately that her favored items already had been covered. She then would apologize for requesting just a "quick little" summary of what had been decided. It was not quick at all because a discussion always followed (and the discussion inevitably resulted in her suggesting changes which improved the results).

Another Chair thought she had a brilliant idea. She would put Late Kate's favorite topics last on the agenda, hoping that would keep Late Kate from leaving early. First, as the previous Chair had discovered, it was not so easy to choose what Kate's favorite agenda items would be. Kate was interested in, prepared well for, and was able to aid the meeting's progress in a constantly surprising array of problems and opportunities. Second, if she saw that an interesting item was scheduled to be taken up after her contemplated leaving time, she would make an irresistible plea for an agenda change. Explaining why she had no choice but to leave early, she begged that those agenda items be shifted to an earlier time. "Please, could we just touch on them very briefly now? Please?"

So with the one severe exception, Late Kate was an unusually good meeting-goer-toer. She lasted a long time, well beyond par, and remained active until her death. Since she lived to almost a hundred, you could say that for once she did not leave early. Of course, when she showed up on high, Saint Peter noted that, as usual, she arrived late.

This completes a sample list of frequent distractions and disruptions that meeting-goer-toers must expect to tolerate. The list is incomplete because the reality is that infinite ways exist to disturb meetings. It is people who do the disrupting, and human beings, we know, are ingenious in discovering ways to aggravate each other. If you aim to be an exceptionally excellent professional in the meetings you attend, please resolve to limit your contributions in the distraction category. Don't do the bad things this chapter has offered as examples. Curb any ambition you find springing up within you to break new ground in the field of meeting disturbing.

Dozers and Dozees

D ozers fall asleep during meetings; Dozees are the fully conscious people attending a meeting with them. Dozees usually are very annoyed, yet sometimes intrigued, by dozers. I wish I could start this discussion by citing some significant statistics about the dozing-during-meetings phenomenon. If only I had realized I would be writing this text and this chapter as I sat in all those meetings I attended. Then I would have made detailed notes about behavior during meetings, put them in my computer, and processed them into elegant observations.

Of course, such note-taking might have hampered my ability to contribute properly during the meetings—I would not have been a good meeting-goer-toer. So, if I am going to ponder at this late stage how I could have prepared better for writing about meetings, I shall have to do so more imaginatively. Let us imagine I have had the benefit of an assistant—someone blessed with both invisibility and a Ph.D. in psychology—who has carefully listened, analyzed, and provided me with clear, incontestable data backing up every point presented in this chapter.

Report on Dozing

That assistant's report, I feel confident, would have presented something like the following specifics:

◇ In any meeting that includes over ten attendees, lasts over twenty minutes, and in which visuals are presented on a screen in a partially darkened room, at least one attendee dozes off.

◇ Some meeting-goer-toers regularly nap during a portion of any meeting they attend and nevertheless continue to be invited to meetings.

◇ Some presenters at meetings manage to put at least one person to sleep shortly after the commencement of their presentations, this independent of other parameters such as subject matter, number of attendees, room size, room lighting, or use of computer displays.

◇ The reasons why dozers doze during meetings is because: (a) they need sleep, or (b) the meeting subject matter is overpoweringly boring, or (c) the speaker—whose combination of voice quality, phrasing, diction, and flow of often-uttered "uh, uh"s is irresistibly hypnotic—holds forth too long, or (d) any assortment of the foregoing.

◇ Of all prevention methods attempted by reluctant about-to-be dozers, the most common, and also the one closest to actually working, is the "hand on cheek pinch."

◇ Dozers, upon suddenly awakening, always try to give the dozees the impression that they really have been awake all the while but purposely closed their eyes so as to listen and concentrate better.

◇ Some dozers, when they come to, immediately ask a question of the speaker, seeking thus to fool the dozees into thinking the dozers have been awake, hence gambling that (a) their question will turn out pertinent to what has transpired just prior to their awakening, (b) the identical question has not already been asked and answered while they were fast asleep, and (c) the speaker to whom the question is addressed is still continuing her presentation and has not been replaced with a different speaker during the dozer's nap.

◇ If a dozer advances to the snoring stage someone sitting next to the snorer willingly elbows or kicks him energetically to awaken him, this being observed favorably by all dozees.

◇ If the boss of a dozer is a dozee at the meeting, the dozee fires the dozer the next day (5 percent of the time), or warns the dozer (20 percent of the time), or plans to take some action but forgets to do it (75 percent of the time).

◇ Some dozees who are themselves borderline dozers will succumb to dozerdom approximately three minutes after a dozer present sets the example.

◇ Though a relatively rare occurrence, some presenters at meetings will actually defy gravity (the social kind) and will become dozers during their own presentations (more precisely, during the question and answer period when a questioner, instead of getting to the question, makes a lengthy introductory speech, a not so rare event).

The foregoing reports by my imaginary assistant tell a useful, real-life story in which all present at meetings where napping occurs should be interested. Some dozing incidents should be judged as very serious and demanding action.

Speaker-Caused Dozing

When you are a speaker at a meeting and you discover someone is sleeping during your talk ask yourself whether you are to blame. If it occurs very infrequently you can be casual about it. You might then reasonably argue that the dozer may have come to the meeting jetlagged from an overseas flight, or was working very late the night before to meet some deadline, or their baby cried all night—circumstances surely related only to the dozer and not to your performance. But what if dozing occurs often, maybe even always, when you speak? What if the entire audience reacts to your

presentation with a swarm of yawns (honest opinions, openly expressed)? You then must face that you are guilty. Your commentating must be very boring and your monotonic voice and speaking style highly sleep-inducing. Perhaps nobody cares what you are talking about and yet you drone on. You take too long to get to the point or when you do the point you are making is of zero interest to your audience.

Have you observed that dozers doze only when you speak and are wide awake during the rest of the meeting? Then no additional evidence is needed for you to conclude that it has to be you. Do you sometimes put your own boss to sleep? Then it is unforgivable if you do nothing. You absolutely have to track down the reasons for the sleeping-pill nature of your meeting contributions. As a first step, may I suggest you reread chapter 4 of this text (on Presentations)?

You, the Dozer

What if you are the dozer? If you tend to lose full consciousness for just a second or two, it may be difficult for you to know if you actually fell asleep. But be assured you have been dozing if you look at the screen and see slide number seventeen and the last slide you recall is number four. What if you hear your name called, and you sense that a question has just been asked though you haven't any idea what it was. What if you look around and realize all the other attendees are looking at you, and you have no idea what is going on? You have been dozing! Realize that!

So what do you do? If you find yourself having difficulty staying awake during any meeting, no matter how seldom, find out why. Is it physical, mental, circumstantial, mysterious? Is it happening more often as time goes on? Has it been occurring for a long time? Be honest!

Do you fall asleep in front of TV? Do you doze off when trying to read a book? Do you have to pull over and nap a while when you attempt a long drive? Worse, a short drive? Are you getting too old to keep going to meetings that don't really interest you that much? Whatever you discover, you must work the problem. A dozer is an "alertness-challenged" meeting-goer-toer, and whatever the reason for his dozing, must be considered a handicapped person within a meeting. Such a handicap is severe. Your dozing is noticed by and annoying to others. Respect for you will be lost. You will not be taken seriously so you will not be assigned important responsibilities. Your career will suffer enormously. You should not let that happen without a fight.

If you feel yourself getting sleepy during a meeting, leave the room for a few moments. Step outside and get some fresh air. Go to the lavatory and splash some cold water on your face. Buy a cell phone that you can set to vibrate (not ring) with an incoming call and get a friend to call you several times during the meeting (and never answer). Rearrange your body in your chair to an uncomfortable position. Finally, pinch your cheek and your thigh frequently.

In anticipation of your encountering the problem, add certain steps in your preparation for the meeting. Plan to be as active in the meeting as possible and get into the discussion frequently. List things for you to bring up and questions for you to ask. Think about any comments from attendees that you might expect and plan either to agree or differ. Do more talking than you usually do because dozers rarely fall asleep in the middle of sentences.

If you cannot figure out why you are a dozer, see a doctor. If he can't help you go see another one. Change your life style if nothing else helps. If you are forced to rate yourself a dozer by nature, ponder realistically what remaining in that mode will do to your life. Never attend a meeting without reminding yourself as you enter the room that if you nod off you may get fired the next day. That thought might help keep you awake.

Your Employer, the Dozee

Now, suppose that you are a dozee and the boss of the dozer. You observe your employee sleeping on the job. You must then do something if for no other reason than that the dozer is cheating—getting paid but not contributing. Before acting consider that something may be wrong with him. Is his dozing partly your fault? Are you working him much too hard? Is he doing too much traveling? Is he on too heavy a schedule? Does he have problems at home? Is he disinterested in the subject under discussion and does that mean he is wrong for his job?

Is he well? Is he an alcoholic? Drinkers, even light ones who start early in the day, find staying awake tough in afternoon meetings. Is he on drugs? If so, are they recreational, habitual, behavior altering? Were they prescribed by a physician? Why? Does your employee ask questions on awakening that prove to everyone that he has been asleep (instead of falsely indicating, as he hopes, that he was awake, as mentioned earlier)? If he gambles in this way then it is unlikely to be his only gambling habit. Do you really want to employ someone who takes such risks with his career?

Some people are born "morning people." They awake early, get going with high energy and spirit, but when lunch is finished so is their pep. They need a nap every afternoon. If they can arrange a lifestyle that allows them to catch a snooze around three or four they will be alert all evening. Such people must avoid afternoon meetings. If you are a Chair engaged in selecting both the attendees and the timing for a forthcoming meeting, don't schedule it for the afternoon if a particular morning person is important to your meeting's success. If you are a morning person and you find yourself dozing during afternoon meetings, don't go to them.

Some meeting-goer-toers, in contrast, are not quite themselves in the morning. Chances are they are "night people;" after dinner they are at their best. Such folks—and we all know some—have to sleep in every morning. It will be unthinking to invite them to morning meetings, still less for those night persons to accept. They will arrive very late for a nine o'clock or not get there at all. If they do show up they will doze.

Dozers and dozees can each learn a lot by studying the actions of dozers and dozees—that is, if they are truly interested in being known as wide awake.

Governing by Meeting

I wrote this book because I believe that holding meetings is the most common means for directing virtually all activities in the American life. We can measure the influence meetings have on our endeavors by the number of meetings held on that subject, and by this measure government operations would win. If you are a government official or a consultant or advisor to government your calendar of scheduled meetings will be excruciatingly tightly crammed. Your day's experiences will be dominated by steady pressure to squeeze in still another meeting, then another and another.

Meetings related to government will encompass all the meeting-going-toing phenomena we have already described as inherent in running businesses, the professions, academics, philanthropy, the performing arts, and anything else. But two potent additional factors magnify the demand for meetings when government is involved. These are bureaucracy and politics, both factors powerful at every government level from the White House down to a town meeting in the smallest village.

As has been discussed earlier, a good fraction of nongovernment meetings are poorly planned and handled and many accomplish little. Still, those private sector meetings tend to be called to deal with specific issues for review and action. In contrast, bureaucracy and politics can cause the very calling of a meeting in government to be an end in itself. The actual announcement of a meeting sometimes is more significant than the meeting. Let us be more specific by example.

The Meeting Is the Message

BUREAU CHIEF'S PLAN FOR THE DAY

Let us say you are in charge of a government group and a problem arises. It is of such a nature that you know you must do something about it right away. Politically it is so serious that you are compelled to at least appear to be tackling it. If you don't respond you may be in big trouble. Also, let us further assume that you know you can't do anything really useful about the issue. Moreover, should you know what ought to be done, you will also know you lack the power to accomplish it. You may possess some of the authority needed to handle the problem, but numerous others in other government bureaus will have to agree with you or they can stand in your way. They not only will have to be, like you, willing to act, but also they must wish to make their input compatible with yours. None of you alone has the power to organize and direct the actions, but you all have review, approval, veto, or other privileges and responsibilities that can either help to move it along or hold it up. We have just described the basic characteristic of bureaucracy: many, many groups and people in on the act. Multiple steps, all difficult to make happen and coordinate, are needed for every decision.

What then do you do? A very common approach is straightforward and will be perceived as proper and effective. You create a committee, a task force, the creation of which is the message. If beneficial results should come from the actual holding of committee meetings, that is a bonus, usually an unexpected one.

We illustrate this with an example at the highest government level. When President Kennedy was assassinated, Lyndon Johnson, the new President, knew he had to take some forceful and conspicuous action immediately regarding that catastrophe, however, there was really nothing he could do. So he appointed a committee to conduct an investigation. In view of the enormity of the tragedy and its profound effect on the nation, he appropriately chose the Chief Justice of the United States Supreme Court to head the group. Only individuals of great prominence were appointed to that task force. President Johnson's creation of the committee was the needed action. What their coming together in meetings could be expected to accomplish was not clear and did not need to be. Though very important in their own worlds, these laypeople lacked the skills to answer the most important questions about the assassination: who had committed the murder, why, and with whose planning and direction? These answers could come only from the work of professional criminal investigators, like the FBI, for whom the task immediately became its top priority. No one really expected much from a group of individuals who had no experience in crime solving. The appointment of the committee was, nevertheless, the expected and necessary act.

Bureaucracy and Politics

Bureaucracy and politics cause government meeting-going-toing to differ from meetings in private sectors, and there are several reasons for this. Almost everything of importance that goes on anywhere—not in government alone—involves numerous interconnections. In nongovernment meetings, however, individual attendees typically will have in mind practical solutions to any questions raised in the meeting. They can expect to come together and develop these with considerable objectivity and competence. They will usually possess adequate decentralized authority for carrying out their mission and they can be expected to move from discussing options to making fairly specific recommendations. Typical meetings in the private sector—say, business corporations' committees, or boards of colleges, or philanthropic organizations' boards—do not usually have to leap high bureaucratic hurdles before they can pursue their agendas.

That is less true in government meetings. Try to get anything in government sensibly planned and activated and you will be surprised how many individuals, bureaus, agencies, and other sources of political interest and political power will turn out to be involved. For one thing, the political aspects of most agenda items in government-called meetings are prominently and actively influential and must be dealt with as front burner items. Meeting attendees must ponder questions like: How will various contemplated actions play with the voters and with the legislative and regulatory bodies? Will the political approvals for actions the meeting has under consideration be obtainable? How does a possible meeting recommendation jibe with what the political parties are pushing? How will the news media respond to the committee's proposals? When disclosed, will the meeting's views affect particular bills now before the lawmaking bodies? Will the committee's deliberations, when made public, have any noticeable effect on coming elections?

The following example, in which I happened to be personally involved, will illustrate the interplay of politics and bureaucracy in government related meetings. Henry Kissinger, after becoming Secretary of State in the second Nixon term in early 1973, created "The Advisory Committee to the Secretary of State for Science and Foreign Affairs." (I was invited to serve on it.) The meetings of this committee pondered such international issues as nuclear weapons proliferation, sharing the oceans' resources, international agreements for positioning space satellites, radio frequency spectrum band allocations, agreements for computerized data and money transfer across borders, and worldwide environmental protection. Kissinger had planned to attend our committee meetings, but he never made it to even one. (No sooner had he established the committee than he had to contend with the breakout of the1973 Arab-Israeli war and with it the possibility of a U.S.–Soviet Union confrontation in the Near East. Then came Watergate and Nixon's resignation. Though that did not involve Kissinger personally, it understandably complicated his schedule).

Having attacked an array of issues that seemed to us extremely important, the committee was concerned that no permanent post existed in the State Department with a continuing responsibility for science-related international matters. So we proposed that there be an Assistant Secretary of State for Science and Foreign Affairs. More than a year of bureaucratic pondering and muddling of the recommendation followed. Such a position was finally created—overcoming the numerous bureaucratic barriers involved—but with the strange and belabored title of Assistant Secretary of State for Oceans and International Environmental and Scientific Affairs. (The naming process itself included several delaying bureaucratic contributions.) When it came time to make the appointment, the White House staff saw the office as providing the opportunity to solve a political appointee problem.

When the energy crisis forced the setting up of ERDA (the Energy Research and Development Administration); the AEC (Atomic Energy Commission) lost its name and independence and its functions were placed within ERDA. The reorganization eliminated the post of Dr. Dixie Lee Ray, a respected scientist, who had headed the AEC till that point. She had some politically influential supporters who hoped she would be chosen to head ERDA. When she was not, the politicos had the idea that she and her admirers would be kept happy with a different prize. She was asked to become the first Assistant Secretary of State for Oceans and International Environmental and Scientific Affairs. She accepted. When she found she was too far back on the waiting list to get in to see the Secretary and also could not obtain approval for the staff and budget she felt necessary, she resigned.

After Jimmy Carter was elected President in 1976, his staff

searched for months for the right Democrat to fill the office—doing so from the political, not the competence, standpoint. They found the answer in Patsy Mink. She had been defeated the previous November for reelection as congresswoman from Hawaii. Her appointment as Assistant Secretary of State for Oceans, etc. gave the state of Hawaii the politically useful public image of "representation" in the Carter Administration. Everyone in the science community was astonished because Mink had no background whatsoever in science or technology. However, she came from the only one of the nation's fifty states totally surrounded by ocean. Thus her appointment to that office tied in well with the word "oceans" in its title and little more.

Though they can be impediments, we should not assume that bureaucracy and politics will strip all government related committees and meetings of their potential usefulness. Instead, the bureaucratic and political dimensions should be regarded merely as handicaps. They stand in the way, but they do not preclude benefits ever being attained. When meetings are run by strong, experienced, and crafty meeting-goer-toers determined to get a job done, they can succeed.

PSAC

After the Soviet Union's Sputnik Earth satellite amazed the world in 1957 there was near panic in some U.S. quarters. The news media suggested the USSR had been highly underrated and now had the lead over us in all science and technology. The American public was shocked, so President Eisenhower had to do something. He acted by using the tried and true formula. He established a committee, the President's Science Advisory Committee (PSAC), whose members were all distinguished scientists. PSAC continued to exist until the Nixon administration. As he saw it, the members of PSAC were naïve and stubborn. Nixon found it annoying that PSAC would arrive at independent views instead of seeing themselves as part of his staff—in other words, they were not properly politically supportive. So Nixon abolished the committee. He was able to do this without approval from the Congress, because PSAC had not been created by the Congress but by executive order.

After Watergate, Nixon's resignation, and Gerald Ford's assumption of the Presidency, Nelson Rockefeller became Vice President (in December 1974). Rockefeller immediately expressed his concern that science and technology competence was missing from the White House team. It was difficult for Rockefeller to imagine any important issue—national security, health, international commercial competitiveness, domestic employment, education, productivity, energy, economic expansion, protecting the environment—that did not possess significant science and technology dimensions.

"It is absolutely unforgivable in this highly technological society of ours," he told me in his office where he invited me to lunch to discuss the matter, "for the White House to neglect science and technology. Carrying out the government's science-and-technology programs should of course be the responsibility of the Defense Department, NASA, the National Science Foundation, and other operating units of the government—but policy and priorities and budget planning regarding such programs need to be set right here, around the President."

But Rockefeller did not suggest that Ford merely reinstate PSAC. He decided to work with Congress to get a proper bill passed. He knew he could get certain Senators and Representatives to agree with him. (He told me he could actually exploit the fact that Nixon had fired the PSAC, because Nixon, as a result of Watergate and the tapes, was then extremely unpopular with both parties.) Rockefeller said that if the Congress made it mandatory by law to have a science and technology office in the White House, then future Presidents might ignore the office but they could not unilaterally abolish it as Nixon had done.

First, Rockefeller succeeded in getting the Congress to pass a bill mandating that there be a temporary group called "the President's Committee on Science and Technology" the membership of which President Ford allowed Rockefeller to choose (and of which I was named chairman). This committee (meeting some half dozen times in the White House with Rockefeller always present and once with President Ford also on hand) then proposed that there be created a permanent office in the White House to be called the Office of Science and Technology Policy. Congress passed a bill in

1975 authorizing this and giving the Office's director a status just below the Cabinet Secretaries.

This particular group of government meetings was hardly typical, of course. Not often can we expect an effort to be commanded by a Nelson Rockefeller. He had, of course, high personal prestige and the contacts and experience to get the task accomplished. He also possessed the interest and determination needed. It is hard for anyone to advance any project in government against the combination of bureaucracy and politics. Even the President of the United States often has to apply every skill and power available to him and his coterie of helpers to get a single bill through Congress or to get Senate approval of an appointment he seeks to make. Too many players become involved in the play as a result of the rules and the culture. But at all stages and all levels there are always "little Rockefellers," people who come to feel that action is needed to accomplish something they strongly believe needs doing. Take the case of young Schroeder.

Bureaucratic Delay

Some years ago, Schroeder was one of the assistants to a Deputy Assistant Secretary somewhere in the Defense Department. He found himself assigned to the task of obtaining from many parts of the DoD the approvals required for creating of a complex new test facility. The officers in charge of the project needed okays for each step (land assignments, purchases of equipment, installations, building and grounds designs, and more.) Each action had to be reviewed by several agencies to be sure no violations of budgets and procedures and no interferences with other projects would occur.

Schroeder soon became convinced that the military project officers involved were up against severe timing pressures. They were very capable and committed, knocking themselves out trying to meet the tough schedules and he was sure they deserved every bit of help he could provide. Alas, with every step he found the numerous administrative groups infuriatingly slow in providing the required approvals. Some simply were lax in even getting to the requests, mainly because they had so many meetings to attend they were seldom in their offices. They were undermanned and had too big a backlog of undone tasks. Others had the habit of routinely questioning everything, always claiming they lacked some additional piece of needed information. They didn't care about getting the project done on time; they just wanted to play it safe, to be sure no one could ever claim they had neglected something. Further delays were caused by Congressional staffers pressing through the bureaucracy for the various contracts to be placed with a supplier in their Congressman's district.

Schroeder decided he absolutely must find a way to accelerate the process. His first attempts were to get the subject of necessary speed-up onto the agendas of the regular "coordination" meetings that abounded in the bureaucracies of DoD and in some overlapping ones elsewhere in the government. These committees were created to encourage greater cooperation among various government agencies, because it was clear that more efficient communication might allow them to work together better.

A GOVERNMENT "COORDINATION" MEETING

The named members of these coordination committees were always fairly high-level. But typically these government executives were totally submerged in urgent problems of the moment. They were often suddenly called away by their superiors to various emergency meetings. They would then send an assistant to represent them at the coordination meetings. These assistants were also swamped, so they often would send their assistants. (In fact, at one meeting, when Schroeder had actually succeeded in getting his problem onto the agenda, he found that none of the attendees had ever met each other, even though that coordination committee had supposedly been holding regular sessions for months). Not surprisingly, he made no progress in accelerating his project through this meeting route.

Schroeder tried next to get his boss, the Deputy Assistant Secretary, to press for urgency with the next level above those in the bureaus with whom he was working. That helped a bit but hurt as much. The lower level people resented being pushed by their bosses because of the pushing he did through his boss. They reacted by slowing things down whenever they could.

So Schroeder decided on a dangerous approach. Without waiting for the actual authorizations to arrive he created by himself the necessary paperwork to enable his military friends to act. Of course, he was well aware he was taking a personal risk. But, he guessed, these acts would not be discovered because the needed signed approvals would arrive eventually. The work would have commenced before the proper papers were in the file, but he figured nobody would bother to look at the files. If someone did probe and found that there were discrepancies between the dates of genuine authorizations and the dates of work starts he had initiated, it would be some time later. He would simply then plead confusion as to why there were inconsistencies here and there in file dates. "I don't know how that happened." This mess-up would be considered as merely the expected par for bureaucratic performance. The risk of his being discovered, he felt, was trivial.

But what if in the review process, the actual approval was withheld on purpose? What if the approval bureaus claimed it to be mandatory that more competitive bids be sought before work could be authorized—and here he had already informed the military they had approval and they had let contracts and work had already begun? In that event he planned to confess. He would say he had been overcome by administrative confusion and, apparently, he had mixed up which items had been approved and which required more steps. He would admit that he had improperly informed the military of approvals before he had actually received them. He would offer to resign. But what, he would ask them, do they now want him to do about it? The angry disapprovers would be reluctant, he bet, to stop the progress. Though unauthorized work was begun though his error, if they were to choose to halt the activity, that would ruin the schedule. Yes, he was to blame, but they would now have to take the blame for schedule delay. He thought they would not want to assume that onus. So they would decide simply to deposit a severely worded reprimand into his personal file and let it go at that.

Of course, they might recommend he be fired. So what? He would relate what he had done to a prospective new employer on the outside who might even rate him higher because he would have proven he could get things done in the government. What he did was not a criminal act so he could not be sent to jail. Anyway, even if they tried to get him fired, only the signature of the Secretary of Defense could effect that. Getting a request for his dismissal to DoD's head would require many steps. The dismissal recommendation would move slowly up the ladder, with long delays at each point. Each individual cosigner would feel it necessary to examine the facts carefully and probably would not ever get around to doing that. In all likelihood the Secretary of Defense would never see the recommendation.

Neither the Rockefeller nor the Schroeder example can be said to be typical of how things work in government because no single way exists. There are the same number of ways to achieve action or inaction in a bureaucracy as there are numbers of people determined to make it happen.

Advisory Committees

The favorite means for managing government operations includes setting up advisory committees in which the main members are nongovernmental. Those members are presumably chosen from among the most highly regarded experts in the country in the committee subject. If you, the reader, has not already been used in this way and if you have attained a reasonable level of recognition as a well-qualified professional in your field, you almost certainly will soon be invited to one or another advisory task force or committee or board at city, county, state, or federal level. If that happens here is some advice:

◇ If the inviter is a high government official don't be flattered by the invitation. Recognize that you may never meet with that person but rather always with one or another assistant.

◇ For some federal advisory boards, Senate approval is required. A Senate staff group will demand a lot of information about you. Investigators may ask your friends and neighbors about your drinking and sex life and whether you're registered as a Democrat or Republican. The disclosures required may include all financial, professional, and personal affiliations (often the same for spouses and close relatives). A detailed list may be demanded of all your assets and liabilities. It's a lot of trouble getting together all the data that they often demand.

◇ If the meeting will include classified information you may need to be "cleared." That process will require even more data, such as a list of every trip you've ever taken out of the country, where precisely you went, why you went, and with whom you met (names, addresses, bios, and affiliations).

◇ Be sure to learn what other "experts" are being invited to be on the committee. Are they really experts or merely associates of some politicians? Don't be amazed if some were chosen for the advisory board for political reasons alone and that they have already been alerted as to what they are to advocate strongly at the meetings.

◇ If some big-wheel names on the board invitation list impress you, consider that they may not accept membership. If they do agree to serve they may never show at a meeting (too busy and too many conflicting meetings because they accept too many advisory committee invitations).

◇ Think about personal risks. For instance, the media may accuse you of a conflict of interest and your reputation may be sullied, especially if you push for what special interest groups may consider the wrong actions.

◇ Will you receive staff briefings? Will you come to realize after the very first meeting that the staff briefing material really constitutes a draft of the final written report you will be expected to cosign eventually?

◇ Beware of work commitments, like your being expected to write a lengthy treatise no one will ever read. Be sure you don't find yourself with an obligation to prepare voluminous material requiring weeks of research and the painful and boring task of negotiating the wording with other meeting participants.

◇ Will you become embroiled in a political controversy or in bureaucratic feuding in which you really are not all that interested?

If pondering the above checklist does not warn you off, then it may well be a privilege for you to accept the invitation and serve diligently. The government needs you—that's for sure. You very likely will accomplish something for your country and will feel good about your participation. In view of the importance of government in our society you cannot rate yourself as a top meeting-goer-toer if you never have participated in government advisory board meetings.

Corporation Board Meetings: Risks and Ethics

Meeting-goer-toers will sometimes find themselves in a meeting and realize they lack the necessary qualification—perhaps knowledge, talent, or experience—to comprehend the matters on the agenda and cannot hope to make a contribution. Even if this seldom happens, it is still disappointing and depressing.

But when it does occur most meeting attendees will feel in no personal danger. The worst result of their incompetence, if noticed by others, might be that they will not be invited to meet with that group again. Meeting participants exposed as inadequate do not usually fear being arrested or taken to court and sued for damages they might have caused. They will not acquire an unanticipated financial liability the settling of which will decimate their net worths. They will not face the possibility of going to jail.

Unless, however, the meeting is of the Board of Directors of a publicly held business corporation that is performing badly. Then, as the saying eloquently goes, all hell can break loose.

Pride and Satisfaction

When a billion-dollar corporation is doing well, its board of directors may reasonably expect rewards for this. You will be viewed as prestigious and valuable, and it is satisfying to know you possess an influence in the running of the nation's economy, something you can certainly claim if you are a director of one of the thousand largest companies in America. You are near the top rungs of the ladder when it comes to having an effect on jobs, living standards, and allocation of the nation's resources. You and your fellow directors are the guardians of the country's strength and well being. You have a right to be proud.

Not only that, you can expect to enjoy the meetings. In them you mix with people who, like you, are very able and are successful because of their abilities. All are experts at something pertinent to managing the business or they would not have been invited onto the board. The company you help lead is prominent and it can be expected to continue to be so because, thanks in part to you, it is well led. The meetings are interesting, and lively question and answer sessions follow presentations on the company's progress. If there are problems, you are part of the group that can and will solve them. The company will have challenging opportunities and the leadership, in which you play a proper role, will grasp them. So being a director and going to board meetings can be rewarding and fascinating, if, as we said, all goes well.

What if everything does not go according to plan? If results fall only a bit short of the expected range, the board will take necessary steps. It may even hire a new CEO if necessary. The owners of the company, the shareholders, will be reasonably tolerant of a few oversights by the board. They will not like it, but they will realize nothing is perfect, so they will accept that results are sometimes disappointing in the world of business. They know a general recession hurts all companies' performances. All in all, the stock owners will patiently allow time for the board to fix things.

Regrettably, in the last several years it has become evident that too many companies have not been competently managed. Actual performances have turned out to be much poorer than was reported to the public. In other words, shareholders have been deceived.

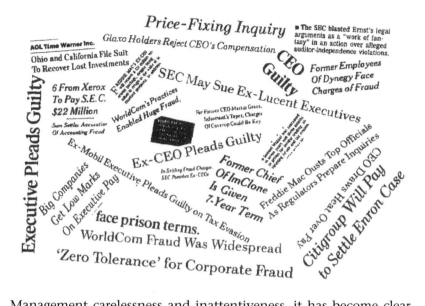

Management carelessness and inattentiveness, it has become clear, have been tolerated and even accepted as par for the business corporation course. Too many corporation executives have been discovered to have been ignorant of falsified accounting and other illegal operations taking place in their companies. Worse, some CEOs, other principal executives, and company directors have been exposed as having planned and gained from criminal activities. High-powered crooks have been discovered in high places in big business.

Directors are expected to know what is going on in the corporations they direct, and they are elected by the stockholders to watch everything. When bad situations occur, the corporation's stock price falls badly and those who bought the shares may be expected to feel mislead and cheated. They may file lawsuits, and in the event that crimes are discovered to have been committed lawsuits are certain. The directors can then be held personally liable. If laws are broken by any company executives, the directors may be seen by both government agencies and shareholders as participants in the criminal actions and hence criminals themselves, thus eligible for punishment.

So, when you walk into a board of directors' meeting as a participant you are a risk taker. If you are a meeting-goer-toer whose activity includes board meetings of publicly traded corporations you must now be totally aware that potential dangers exist as well as potential rewards. Balancing the good and the bad is critical. We explore this further.

The Compensation Committee

Imagine that you are a director of a corporation we shall call "Typical Corp., Inc.,"[5] and you are attending a meeting of the board of directors of that company. It is the annual meeting when the compensation of the CEO is to be decided by the board. The chairman and CEO is Wilson, the president and chief operating officer is Watkins, and the chairman of the compensation committee of the board is Wallace. At the point in the meeting when the CEO's remuneration is the next agenda item, Wilson steps out of the boardroom and Wallace becomes the Chair temporarily.

Wallace brings in the vice president for human relations and the head of a consulting firm specializing in executive compensation. Together they make a presentation that summarizes the study they have made of the CEO compensation in comparable other corporations. Now, to begin with, although Wilson is not present, as an experienced and sophisticated director you know that he knows precisely what the vice president and the consultant will report and what they will recommend to the board. Wilson, approved, if he did not actually create, their script. You also know that Wilson has chosen that vice president who, of course, reports to Wilson. Wilson determines that vice president's remuneration. Also, Wilson has chosen the consultant and negotiated his fee. Furthermore, you are aware that the consultant would like to retain Typical Corp. as a well-paying client and enjoy the income from performing the same task next year.

The presenters describe to the board the average CEO compensation in the five companies they have selected as most qualified to be regarded as "peers." You figure there are perhaps twenty-five companies they have looked at as being in some ways similar to Typical Corp. The five finalists they have very carefully chosen,

---

[5] This corporation is nonexistent. Yet it is not totally fictitious. I have simply synthesized the characteristics of three real companies in Typical Corp., Inc., to help make this presentation of typical non-praiseworthy practices of many executives.

you are inclined to guess, are probably those with the highest CEO pay (counting salary, bonus, stock options, pensions, etc.). You make this assumption because in your own company that is the accepted practice. Moreover, informal discussions in the "CEO club" confirm that this is what virtually every company does. This is especially so when the companies ask for help from a consulting firm that specializes in this corporate executive remuneration area.

It also comes as no surprise to you when the recommendation made to the board by Wallace, seconded by Watkins, is for a very substantial increase in Wilson's overall compensation. This is after the report is made that he has been found to be below the average of the CEO's pay in the five comparable companies. Nor is it amazing when the board accepts the recommendation and approves the raise unanimously.

Now it happens that this year's profit performance of Typical Corp. is well below last year's and, moreover, that a downward "restatement" of previously announced revenues and earnings for past years is being made ready for public announcement. This decrease in reported results, it is claimed, was not the result of any act or omission by the CEO but rather because of internal accounting blunders not caught by the outside auditing firm. Worse, an investigation is underway by the SEC (Securities Exchange Commission) to establish whether these mistakes were really errors or deliberate and improper acts to inflate reported earnings.

Of the various members of the board, it is worth our noting that three are CEOs of other companies and that Wilson happens to be a board member of all three of those companies. Wilson thus votes on the compensation of those companies' CEOs just as they, as directors of Typical Corp., vote on his. Their companies also hire that same consulting firm to study the compensation of CEOs of comparable companies. Other directors on the Typical board should also be mentioned. One is the CEO of the bank that is Typical's leading banker. Another is the managing partner in the law firm Typical employs and is the firm member assigned to direct that firm's work for Typical. The third director is the managing partner of the large accounting firm that provides the outside audit of Typical. That accounting firm also has a consulting division that is paid generously by Typical to help it find ways to minimize taxes and maximize reported sales and earnings. This consulting work is considered very important because much of what is ethical and legal is a matter of judgment and so it is manifestly valuable to employ "outside" judgments in arriving at the best figures.

Three other directors are the Typical Corp.'s three leading operating executives, namely, the president, the chief financial officer, and the executive vice president.

Now, what is wrong with Typical Corp.'s board and the compensation meeting we have described? Several things stand out as improper and questionable if not out-and-out atrocious. (Some are not now allowed by the pertinent U.S. government regulatory agencies nor by new accounting standards rules.) Let's look at this further.

Overpaid CEOs

The board of directors of Typical Corp., Inc., raised CEO Wilson's pay substantially even though the company's performance was much poorer than the previous year's. It is no excuse that the boards of other corporations were engaging in the same practice.

Every CEO in all of those other companies was determined by its board to be earning less than the CEOs of peer companies. All the directors were totally aware that this fantasy formula for determining CEO remuneration was escalating all CEO remunerations as each board annually raised its CEO pay to "catch up" with other CEOs' pay. All directors involved, we see, obviously were members of the same "CEO Saluting" club.

If you read business news you will have noted that the CEO of a company known as Tyco is under indictment for looting his company. Yet, between annual compensation and the termination pay granted him when he was finally fired, he netted over eighty million dollars, the second highest remuneration of any CEO in 2002! How could the Tyco directors have allowed this? How could they have so risked their reputations and their personal net worths?

Unfortunately the Tyco case is not the exception. Fortune magazine published the average CEO compensation of the Standard and Poor's list of the five hundred largest corporations and noted it rose 14 percent in 2002 while the total return to shareholders dropped 22 percent.

Recently, a company seen as failing was purchased for a pittance by another company. All of the directors, and especially the CEO, nevertheless received enormously generous termination payments—amazingly improper rewards for leading a company to have no choice but to sell out at a bargain price or collapse. They probably shouldn't have been surprised when they were promptly sued by the holders of the common stock, the value of which had declined disastrously under their leadership.

As a board member you must regularly apply serious judgment to CEO remuneration decisions. If you are not prepared to do that then you will fail in several ways. One is not seeing the danger to yourself. You may be taken to court and asked to compensate shareholders for their losses resulting from your laxity. You may expect to be accused of participating in and profiting from the unethical practices. You and the CEO may be regarded as fellow connivers in arranging that all of you be overpaid.

In recent years shareholders, both small individual owners of stock and large institutional investors, have become angry about what is seen as the excessive CEO remunerations. The combination of salaries, bonuses, options, perks, termination packages, and retirement plans have been adding up to several tens of millions per year for the top executives. This has happened even when they are being or should be dismissed for incompetence because of terrible company performance or after the discovery of unethical, sometimes fraudulent, actions on their part. Such awards are now regarded as vulgarly huge, obviously wrong, and the equivalent of piggish grand larceny against the owners of the company. If you are a director who goes to a board meeting and approves such awards, you and your fellow members must accept the responsibility for allowing this unacceptable condition to develop and continue to exist. You should expect to be punished.

The Shareholder's Representative

Earlier, we asked you to imagine you were a director of Typical Corp., Inc., attending a board meeting; nothing in the description of that meeting suggested that you were concentrating on what was in the best interest of the company's shareholders. Legally, as a director of a corporation, you go to a board meeting to represent the shareholders. They elected you to do exactly that. But as a practical, real-life matter, this duty will not always be dominant in your mind as a you participate in corporate board meetings. For one thing, while your having been voted on to the board of directors by the shareholders is a fact, it is only technically so. It isn't as though your name was put forth by a large band of shareholders who, knowing your background and capabilities, sought you out as their candidate. Actually, it was the very board of directors to which you were elected a member that nominated you. Most often, in fact, the CEO composes a list of candidates and submits it to the board. The board, without discussion, simply approved that choice routinely and unanimously.

Again technically, the CEO works for and reports to the board which has the power and responsibility to appoint the chief executive officer. The board can fire the CEO yet in most cases the CEO has chosen the board members. If this seems an illogical and absurd example of mutual back scratching of authorities and responsibilities, it is. Someone with no detailed knowledge of how American big business works might expect that this seemingly nonsensical arrangement of conflicting, overlapping and self-anointed authorities would cause most of the big American companies to be always in serious trouble. However, only a few of these corporations are performing so badly at any given time as to call into question the relation of directors to CEOs and to shareholders. The director election system in truth works well for the vast majority of corporations if only because there is no obviously better and more functional alternative.

How can you as a director represent the shareholder better than to rely on a CEO you helped choose and whom you believed to be competent? You and your fellow directors can replace that chief executive if the company's performance is unsatisfactory. Similarly, how can the shareholders select a better slate of directors to represent them than the slate presented to them by the company's management, even if in truth that may mean chosen by the CEO alone? It is not always helpful to you to be preoccupied by your responsibilities to your shareholders as the board meetings' agendas unfold. Instead, concentrating on seeing that the corporation is well managed and thus successful is a better conceptual aid.

Thus, constantly judging the CEO's ability, ethics, and firmness in law obeisance is the most realistic definition of the true role of a corporation's director. To accomplish this is not easy. At every board meeting you attend as a director you should have the following in the front of your mind:

◇ The CEO may not know with sufficient depth what is going on in the company. The corporation may be heading for disaster and the CEO may not realize it.

◇ The performance figures you review at board meetings may not be accurate or sound. They may be based on improper, even illegal, accounting and reporting. You cannot trust 100 percent what the CEO and the other senior executives tell you.

◇ The outside accountants the corporation has hired may not be doing a proper job.

◇ The corporation may be badly behind competitors and you are not being accurately informed of its competitive position.

◇ The corporation may be so highly mismanaged that you may need to search for a new CEO.

◇ Don't become a close personal friend of the CEO or other principal executives of the company.

Keeping such thoughts on your brain's front burner during every meeting will be your best way of being a director representing the shareholders, however you become a director.

Conflicts of Interest

If you are headed for a meeting of the board of a corporation listed on the stock exchanges, ask yourself if you have a conflict of interest. That is something the directors of Typical Corp., Inc., were not in the habit of doing. The disclosure of accounting frauds, the parade of corporations admitting to having falsified their reporting earnings as they restated them later, the overcompensation of CEOs, and other sins of the managers of corporations has led to heightened determination both by the U.S. government and the shareholders to prohibit management patterns that can allow such happenings. For example, it has been common in the past for a substantial fraction of the directors to also be operating executives of the company. This was true of Typical Corp., whose board included the president, the chief financial officer, and the executive vice president. As such they certainly each have a conflict of interest. They report to, work for, and are hired by the boss, the CEO. Yet, if those executives are also board members that says the CEO reports to them. Are we seriously to assume the CEO may be dismissible by individuals whom the CEO can dismiss? Isn't that nonsense? It is a conflict of interest when directors' personal aims are served by their catering to the person to whom they report rather than to the owners of the corporation who have elected them as their representatives? It is high time that such foolishness ceases to be tolerated by shareholders and by the SEC, the federal government's agency that exists to oversee corporations and prevent just such clear conflicts of interest.

A concept gaining momentum now is that all directors should be "independent," and that other than the CEO no director may be an employee of the company. What about allowing bankers, lawyers, accountants, and certain other professionals to serve on the board? If the corporation is using the banker's bank or the lawyer's firm and the accountant's firm, those directors will have obvious conflicts of interest. When they sit in a board meeting and an agenda item is under discussion they cannot be expected to think solely of the shareholder's interest. How will the handling of every item effect their being retained and paid well for the service they now render the corporation? Won't they seek to please the CEO who can dismiss them thus negatively influencing their personal incomes? If they believe the way to go in the interest of the corporation's owners is different from the way the CEO wishes the decision of the board to be, will they vote against the CEO?

Director Competence

How do you reconcile the obvious benefits of independent directors with the need for the company to have directors with experience in the corporation's primary business? For one thing, the

CEO of a corporation should never serve on the board of any company that employs any of his directors as its CEO. That director cannot be independent because the CEO and that director each help to set each other's remuneration. No need to say more.

How about having an executive from a company producing bananas serving as director of a company producing auto parts, with no other connections. That banana expert, it would appear, could be categorized as a truly independent director of the auto-parts company. But is that relevant? Would you as a stockholder of the auto-parts company really want to have someone exert a major influence on the value of your stock whose expertise has to do with bananas and not auto parts? Wouldn't you want all your directors to possess knowledge, experience, and a success record in activities somewhat close to the business of the auto-parts company you own?

But if the director has these qualifications doesn't that mean that a conflict of some sort might exist? After all, that director would have had to obtain or is now accumulating auto parts competence somewhere somehow, probably with a competitor. Even if he is no longer an employee or a consultant to other competitive companies, that director might still own stock in or receive pension income from such companies. Thus the director is not totally independent. Does the director have a close friendship with one of your operating executives (thus inclined to vote the way that executive might wish her to vote, in a way favorable to him but not the shareholders)?

An expert in accounting can be useful in any business. A top accountant, like a top business lawyer, or a professor of business administration, has abilities suitable for useful participation in a meeting of the board of directors of many companies. True, of course, but corporations specifically hire such experts to do their specialized tasks as needed. You do not expect the directors to perform duties you hire specialists to provide. Besides, your accountant will likely have some present or past association with an accounting firm that would like to do your accounting.

Seeking total "so-called" independence of directors can be carried too far. If you become, or continue to be, a director of a corporation, the reward/risk ratio of your position must always be on your mind. Shareholders should expect that to ensure competence in the director's group may require their accepting some small degree of possible but actually remote and very trivial conflict of interest. As a director you cannot expect perfection from yourself in the matter of independence. You must feel you can risk the penalties if the company performance is unsatisfactory and considered to have resulted in part because you had a conflict of interest with the company. Assess the degree to which you fall short of, or will be accused of not being, independent. If you believe that extent to be minor, take a chance. It's a matter of potential benefits versus possible penalties.

Director Incompetence

In the future, directors will not rely on the CEO to uncover all errors, whether they were due to carelessness, lack of expertise, or criminal intent. To imagine the directors or the CEO should know everything is unrealistic. In a billion-dollar corporation there are thousands of daily decisions involving hundreds of details. For those decisions, judgments are required as well as specialized knowledge of law and accounting rules. Thus, the only way a corporation of substantial size can hope to operate is with massive decentralization of authority and responsibility. Each level, as it integrates the data of money flow, product production, incoming materials, wages payment, customer billing, and the rest, must rely on the inputs received from various company operators. Of course, internal auditors exist to make continuous checks, but they might realistically be expected to catch half of the big errors, a tenth of small ones, and a tiny fraction of errors of judgment (which would really represent mere differences of opinion with no certainty as to who is right). No CEO or board member can expect to be in a position to vouch for the quality of the information in masses of data.

It is not simply a matter of having accurate numbers. Performance figures for a corporation depend on a huge number of individual decisions for which clear criteria do not always exist. Example: a company has acquired a patent for twenty-five million dollars. It was purchased because the executives with the authority to make such purchases believed the profit generated in exploiting that patent would greatly exceed the purchase price. But suppose some other firm suddenly claims it holds an earlier patent that supercedes the company's purchased patent, making the latter worthless. Suppose also that an initial examination does not make clear whether the outside claim has merit. Instead, it looks as though a long and substantial study will be required to be sure.

How should the company handle the disclosure of this situation? Should it assume that the outside claim is sound and therefore announce a twenty-five-million-dollar loss? If it does this, some shareholders will sell their falling stock and take a loss. But what if the purchased patent is later upheld, a great profit stream results, and the stock soars? Might not those who sold low and missed the rise have a basis for suing the directors for misleading them by a wrong early announcement? Could they not claim the directors "should have known" the outside claim was without merit and the patent good?

Conversely, what if the company delays the announcement and then has to announce a twenty-five-million-dollar loss months or years later when it becomes certain the patent is no good, and the stock then falls? Won't the shareholders who bought stock earlier sue because they wouldn't have purchased shares knowing that information?

Imagine this kind of judgment call happening time and again on numerous big and little items every day. It is easy to see that expecting the top management to have information and be right in their judgment about everything that can happen is to dream. Yet shareholders demand that their corporate officers and directors think and act perfectly, and the intensity of these demands will only grow in years to come.

The Dictator

Small companies are often run by the dictates of a single all-powerful executive. He may be the founder and sole owner of the company. If it is a corporation, the stock will likely be closely held by that leader or perhaps by a few financial backers. Even a very large corporation can find itself with a board chairman who becomes a dictator, a central figure who dominates everything. His executive staff are yes-men chosen by him alone. The members of the board of directors have all been put in place by the CEO and expect to have little influence. The dictatorial chairman, being the sole, all-powerful decision-maker, doesn't even try to keep the board well informed and no one questions that. For a dictator-run company it is even more unrealistic to imagine the CEO can "know everything."

Once management takes on a dictator style it is unlikely to change until the company's performance is seen to deteriorate badly and often even well beyond that point. Sadly the likelihood of that downturn happening is great. It is delayed if the general economy is growing and the stock market is booming. When those favorable conditions cease to exist, the dictator's company will suffer substantially more than competitive companies with a more broadly capable top echelon of management. This is for a number of reasons, such as:

◇ The dictator will get less help than he needs from the members of the board and from his executive staff, as he is in the habit of holding the power in his hands alone.

◇ The members of the board of directors and his principal executives will be of mediocre competence. Really capable people will not serve under and be subservient to a dictatorial leader.

◇ The dictator, no matter how smart, is not smart enough to encompass by himself all the knowledge and ideas needing integration to make good decisions. Thus the company will make more mistakes and overlook more opportunities than better run companies effectively employing a team approach to management.

◇ A large company is dependent not only on what is generated within it but on what happens outside it. A CEO who is regarded as an egotist—why else would he believe it is wise for him to manage his company as a dictator—is not popular with and not sought out by other business leaders. He is not favored with exposure to a wide spread of views, ideas, and information from his peers around the world.

◇ The dictator, being in full charge, and esteeming his abilities to be so remarkable as not needing others for major decision-making, is likely to greatly overpay himself in salary, bonuses, stock options, and undisclosed favors. He acts as though he owns the company, not the shareholders. As that leaks out, and it eventually does, this causes the company to be rated down by investors, financial firms, and the business media.

This book has urged that meeting-goer-toers, when considering joining a board of directors or renewing such membership, continually assess the risk to reward ratio. If you believe the board in question reports to a dictator, you should lower your estimate of the benefits to you. Being a director and going to board meetings won't be much fun; you will derive few satisfactions and little prestige, and you will be at a very high risk.

The Coming Revolution

The public, the relevant government agencies, the accounting firms, shareholder groups, and employees of corporations now believe that management mishaps have become far worse than is tolerable. So in the decade ahead the rules for directors and managers of large publicly held corporations are bound to undergo huge changes. The obligations of the board members to the shareholders will be made clearer and tighter. Superior criteria for realistically assessing conflicts of interest will be worked out. Demands for greater competence and ethical behavior by corporate leaders will grow and that will force change.

To meeting-goer-toers, I suggest then that to be a member of the board of a publicly held corporation during the next decade will be fascinating. As constantly urged in this chapter, you must carefully examine the risks of being a director. Do not get caught going to board meetings where you are supplied with less knowledge than you should have. Don't join a board if you have a real conflict of interest. Don't pay the CEO excessively or allow him or her to overcompensate you as a reward for your engaging in such overcompensation.

In summary, when you go to a corporation meeting, do not make the classic mistakes that will lead to your being punished for your actions. Be highly ethical, informed, and determined to be a good director. Approach directorship in this way and you will have an invigorating and exciting experience. Your participation in the coming cultural revolution of American corporations' boards of directors will be one of the defining experiences of your business life.

About the Author

Simon Ramo, born in Salt Lake City, Utah, received a Ph.D. magna cum laude from the California Institute of Technology at age twenty three. Early a prominent pioneer in electronics research and development, he received the nation's highest science award, the National Medal of Science. Ramo became a major figure in the technology for national defense, including serving as the chief scientist and technical director of the U.S. Intercontinental Ballistic Missile (ICBM) program, the country's largest defense project, and was awarded the Presidential Medal of Freedom, the U.S.'s highest civilian award. Ramo's books on science, engineering, and management are used in universities throughout the world. A founder and principal executive of several successful hi-tech companies, he was inducted into the Business Hall of Fame. He was influential in arranging Northrop-Grumman's acquisition of TRW (Thompson Ramo Wooldridge) and is Senior Consultant to the CEO of Northrop-Grumman.

Now ninety two, Ramo estimates he has attended over forty thousand meetings in his lifetime—corporate directors, symphony boards, university trustees, baseball Little Leagues, government advisories, philanthropy foundations—thirty thousand of which, he has concluded, could have been shorter with more useful results or need not have been held.